W9-ATJ-667

WORLD

MYSTERIES REVEALED

MICHAEL BRADLEY

BARNES & NOBLE

NEW YORK

Additional copyrighted information appears on p. 160

Published exclusively for Barnes & Noble, Inc., by Gusto Company.

© 2005 GUSTO Company As

Written by Michael Bradley with Ted Streuli
Illustrations by Zooid Ltd
Executive Editors and original concept by James Tavendale and Ernesto Gremese
Edited by James Tavendale and Stephen Lynn
Designed by Jeffrey Swartz

ISBN 0-7607-7222-3

05 06 07 08 09 M 9 8 7 6 5 4 3 2 1

CONTENTS

WARNING

Restricted Area

It is unlawful to enter this area without permission of the Installation Commander.

Sec. 21, Internal Security Act of 1950; 50 U.S.C. 797

While on this Installation all personnel and the property under their control are subject to search.

Use of deadly force authorized.

INTRODUCTION

Everyone loves a good mystery. Here are over twenty of the world's greatest—exposed and explored. For years they have eluded explanation, baffling skeptics and believers alike. All have attracted their fair share of quacks, crackpots, and conspiracy theorists.

The truth is rarely simple. It isn't "out there." It lies, instead, in that gray area between the "official" government or "scientific" explanation and the sometimes-ludicrous flights of fancy that seem to dissolve under close scrutiny.

This book covers a wide spectrum of intriguing enigmas, from strange talents and outer-space phenomena to monsters of the ocean and land creatures that evade capture. It probes the spirit world, experiments with magnetism, and the time-space continuum; it scrutinizes the achievements of ancient civilizations, extraterrestrials, powers beyond human understanding, miracles, magic, and mysteries. All of these phenomena plus many more perplexing riddles are explored.

We ask important questions, then attempt to address both sides of the argument so that you get the chance to suspend disbelief and open your mind to the fascinating possibilities that surround us. We seek neither to dream nor debunk, but rather to sift through all the facts and fictions, placing gripping alternatives side by side, often for the first time. We invite you to keep an open mind and reveal some startling new conclusions *they* don't want you to know.

ALIENS

In May 2001, a gathering of the world's press in Washington, D.C., was presented with the testimony of Dr. Steven Greer and twenty-one witnesses from his Disclosure Project—a nonprofit research project working to fully disclose the facts about UFOs, extraterrestrial intelligence, and classified advanced energy and propulsion systems. In total, more than 400 witnesses have signed up to Greer's project. Most are high-ranking figures in the worlds of politics, the military, or NASA. Many are breaking oaths of secrecy. All claim to have firsthand experience of an alien presence on earth.

Is there reliable evidence of an alien presence on earth?

YES! There have been recorded interactions with aliens on earth since ancient times. Ancient texts from Egypt, India, China, and elsewhere make reference to flying gods in fiery chariots or flying boats. Ancient Buddhist texts refer to flying spheres. Many early civilizations believed man descended from, and returned to, the stars and the strange "gods" that lived there.

NO! For the people of ancient civilizations, the skies did hold a fascination, but not because of aliens that descended from them. Rather, the sun's heat, and its apparent movement across the sky, the mysteriousness of the stars, and the cycles of the moon were powerful visual factors in daily life. It is hardly surprising, then, that the religious beliefs of the ancients incorporated astro-

YES! Archaeological evidence has uncovered skeletal remains and other artifacts that suggest early man was in regular contact with aliens. In 1938, in the Baian Kara Ula Mountains on the Tibetan border, cave drawings were discovered that illustrate figures in helmets and depict the solar system. Ancient Sumerian texts, as translated by Zecharia Sitchin in *The Earth Chronicles*, describe a tenth planet in our solar system, known in Sumerian as Nibiru, from which aliens came and lived on earth, even interbreeding with humans. (A tenth planet, Sedna, was indeed identified in 2003.)

The Ica Stones of Peru bear depictions of humanoid figures interacting with dinosaurs and even performing complex medical procedures. They have been dated to the Mesozoic Period, 230 million years ago, long before humans walked the earth. Fossilized footprints found in Southwest America support this as they date back 250 million years.

There are hundreds of reliable eyewitness accounts of UFO sightings in more recent times. The Disclosure Project has 400 witnesses, selected entirely on their strong credentials. Among them are NASA personnel who describe regulations that restrict them from passing on information concerning UFO sightings in space.

NASA personnel routinely airbrush out UFOs from satellite images of the earth from space. Many astronauts have reported direct encounters with UFOs in space. Major Gordon Cooper flew solo in a space capsule as part of the Mercury flights in 1963. He reported seeing a brightly shining UFO coming directly towards him, which the control center in Muchea, Australia, was able to track on radar.

It is arrogant to assume that Earth is the only populated planet when there is an abundance of other planets in countless galaxies.

Eyewitness accounts of alien abductions from all over the globe contain many similarities, indicating that there is an essence of truth

N O ! nomical mysteries in order to make sense of their world. Here lies the origin of references to flaming chariots and fire-breathing dragons (the sun). It is not evidence of aliens.

The argument that archaeology provides evidence of an alien input into man's earliest civilizations was most enthusiastically purported by Erich von Däniken in *Chariots of the Gods? Unsolved Mysteries of the Past*. This has not earned him the respect of mainstream archaeologists; indeed, some of his evidence was fraudulent, while the rest was unfounded and erroneous. His theories also depended upon ancient civilizations being feeble, primitive, and in dire need of the intervention of a more intelligent species. This is clearly not the case.

The Ica Stones are carved for the tourist trade. If such an advanced alien race came to earth so long ago, why did they resort to such a primitive method of recording their presence here?

The vast majority of eyewitness sightings of UFOs are not reliable. Weather conditions, meteors, military aircraft, and reflections of light off birds and aircraft account for these sightings. How mysterious would highly advanced aircraft such as the modern stealth bomber have appeared if sighted in public during its top-secret early days? Tiny movements of the eye can also make a stationary light appear to be moving in what psychologists call the auto-kinetic effect.

Abduction by aliens is a fictitious phenomenon, inspired by early science fiction such as H. G. Wells novels and the Buck Rogers comic strips of the 1930s. The popularization of the first abduction accounts has created a global delusion of false memory, often extracted from the "subconscious" via hypnosis. Despite the several hundred individuals who claim to have undergone this experience, not a single one has produced a spacecraft artifact. People who claim to have been subjected to some kind of alien implants turn out

YES! in the phenomenon. Most abductees report the incident happening at night as they were sleeping; being transported through walls and windows with ease; and undergoing some sort of medical procedure. Many women claim they were artificially inseminated. All describe an immense terror, but many were reassured by the calming telepathic communications of their abductors. The scale of the reports worldwide suggests that there has to be some basis in truth.

The growing evidence that suggests a government conspiracy to conceal alien contact and UFO sightings worldwide is also indicative that contact has been made. The Roswell story in 1947 was the most famous incident to spark public mistrust in the government and raise suspicion of a cover-up. Several civilians were the first to witness the alien aircraft that crashed in the desert, but as soon as military personnel arrived at the scene, the evidence was swiftly removed, and all eyewitness accounts were refuted. The cover-up had begun. Now Dr. Greer is staging a major campaign to pressure the U.S. government to disclose all files relating to UFO sightings and alien contact that his reliable witnesses assert are being stored secretly in the name of national security.

Sightings suggest the superior technological capability of alien visitors, and some argue that governments have secretly learned from this technology. Greer's eyewitnesses affirm that reverse engineering of crashed UFO crafts has already equipped the government with the wherewithal to provide the Earth with alternative, renewable, and emission-free energy sources. He wants the government to act now to implement these energies across the world so as to avert a global catastrophe.

N O ! to have something entirely more organic lodged in their nasal cavity.

The conspiracy theory myth has been perpetuated by Hollywood. Movies such as *Close Encounters of the Third Kind* (1977) resulted in a wave of urban mythology relating to Roswell. The secrecy necessary for the testing of new military aircraft in sites such as Area 51 does nothing to help suppress this irrational fear. D. H. Rawcliffe has described Roswell as an example of "retrospective falsification."

YES!

CONCLUSION:

1. There is ample evidence that aliens have been visiting the earth for centuries.

2. There are reliable eyewitnesses to this phenomenon.

3. There is sufficient correlation between alien abduction reports to suggest they share a common truth.

4. The growing evidence of government conspiracy to conceal details of alien encounters and UFO sightings suggests that there is indeed something worth hiding.

Recommended reading

Hancock, Graham. *Fingerprints of the Gods: The Evidence of Earth's Lost Civilization*. Three Rivers Press, 1996.

Korff, Kal K. *The Roswell UFO Crash: What They Don't Want You to Know*. Dell, 2000.

Marrs, Jim. *Alien Agenda: Investigating the Extraterrestrial Presence Among Us*. Harper Torch, 1998.

Sitchin, Zecharia. *The Twelfth Planet: Book I of the Earth Chronicles*. Avon, 1999.

Von Däniken, Erich. *Eyes of the Sphinx: The Newest Evidence of Extraterrestrial Contact in Ancient Egypt*. Berkley, 1996.

N O !

CONCLUSION:

1. There is no reliable evidence of the existence of aliens.

2. Mainstream archaeology does not support the view that ancient civilizations lived with an alien race.

3. Modern UFO sightings are commonly of natural meteorological phenomena or can be otherwise explained.

4. Alien abduction accounts are fabricated or are the result of a delusional personality.

5. There is no evidence of a conspiracy to conceal evidence of aliens on earth.

Recommended reading

Bullard, Thomas E. "Ancient Astronauts." *The Encyclopedia of the Paranormal,* edited by Gordon Stein. Prometheus Books, 1996.

Feder, Kenneth L. *Frauds, Mysteries and Myths.* McGraw Hill Co., 2001.

Frazier, Kendrick (editor), Karr, Barry (editor), and Nickell, Joe (editor). *The UFO Invasion: The Roswell Incident, Alien Abductions, and Government Cover-ups.* Prometheus Books, 1997.

Story, Ronald. *Guardians of the Universe.* St. Martin's Press, 1980.

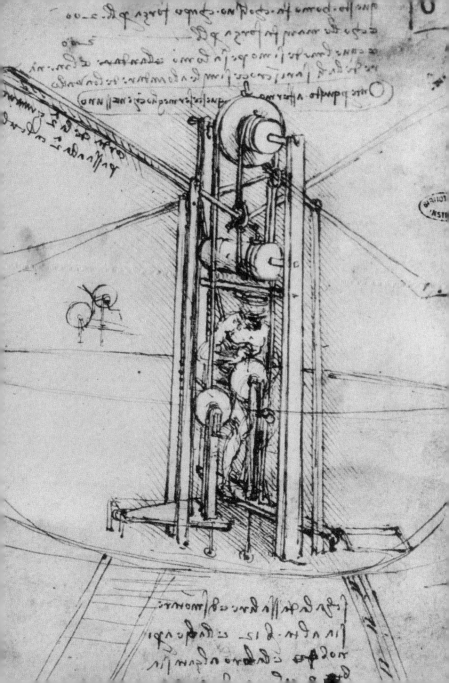

ANCIENT FLYING MACHINES

Modern man prides himself on his scientific and technological developments. His knowledge and understanding of the universe is advancing rapidly, and his feats of engineering grow ever more astounding.

The notion of men flying was once hailed as an absurd dream, but one of modern man's greatest achievements is the invention of the airplane. However, some believe that modern man was not the first to conquer the skies.

Did the ancients get there first?

YES! An object bearing an uncanny resemblance to a modern airplane was found in a tomb in Saqqara, Egypt, in 1898. It was determined to be nearly 2,000 years old. As modern airplanes had yet to be invented, the object was put into a box and labeled "wooden bird." It was rediscovered in 1969 by Dr. Khalil Messiha, who noted the

NO! Although the theory of heavier-than-air flight was mooted as far back as the thirteenth century, and although Leonardo da Vinci produced amazingly detailed diagrams of winged aircraft, it wasn't until 1903 that man achieved his dream of powered flight.

On December 17, 1903, Wilbur and Orville Wright success-

YES! amazing similarities between the model and advanced forms of "pusher gliders." The model also had unusually curved wings, similar to those of the Concorde. A committee of eminent scientists authenticated the object, and it was put on display in the Cairo museum labeled "model airplane."

To build a flying device with such advanced features would require an in-depth knowledge of aerodynamics. The ancient Egyptians are credited as being a highly developed civilization.

The ancient Egyptians often built scale-models of devices they planned to construct.

Hundreds of miles south of Cairo, at a place called Abydos, images of modern-day aircraft were found carved into the ceiling of a 3,000-year-old temple. They are remarkable representations of helicopters, gliders, and jet planes.

Gold objects found in a tomb in Colombia, estimated to be at least 1,000 years old, are strongly reminiscent of modern aircraft, and have many mechanical features. One of the objects in particular looks astonishingly like an airplane. It has a fuselage, elevons (wing flaps), and a tail-fin that is the exact shape of fins on modern airplanes.

There are thousands of references to flying machines in ancient Indian texts. These machines were called *vimanas,* and were either saucer-shaped or cylindrical. They were able to travel within the Earth's atmosphere or under water, and were often used in warfare.

When Alexander the Great invaded India it is recorded that his armies were attacked by "flying fiery shields."

In 1875, an ancient text written by Bharadvajy the Wise was rediscovered in a temple in India. The text, dating back to the fourth century B.C., speaks extensively of the *vimanas*, giving instructions

N O ! fully flew the first engine-powered airplane. Their achievement was the culmination of a lifelong fascination with every aspect of flying. They studied every paper ever written on aeronautics and devised countless experiments to test their theories. The breakthrough came after the brothers built a pilot-less kite and became convinced they could construct an aircraft "capable of sustaining a man."

Although the Ancient Egyptians were clearly capable of many things, there is no record of them ever having experimented with kites or balloons, which would have been the logical precursor to inventing a flying machine.

Of all the ambiguous artifacts purported to be models of ancient flying machines, none have been categorically identified as such. Indeed, scientists have labeled these objects as *zoomorphic* (animal-shaped).

There are many types of winged animals, such as birds, bats, insects, and some species of fish. It is reasonable to assume that ancient civilizations made models of these creatures. Many were depicted as lifelike, but others were more crude representations, and some were plainly abstract.

One of the most contested ancient objects bearing a strong resemblance to a modern airplane was sent for analysis to aerodynamics experts. They pointed out that there were several features that were inconsistent with the object being a model for an aircraft. The wings were in the wrong position, and the nose would have been unworkable in an aircraft.

No physical remains of ancient Indian aircraft have been found, which seems strange if they were so abundant.

YES! for their operation. It includes precise details on how to steer the flying machines and how to switch the drives from a free energy source to solar energy.

The free energy source used to fuel ancient flying machines is said to be "anti-gravity," and based upon the power of *laghima*. *Laghima* is the ancient art of controlling the effect of Earth's gravity on oneself and is used in levitation. Ancient documents recently discovered in Tibet and translated at the Chandrigarh University detail the use of this energy in propelling flying machines.

The *Rig Veda* is the oldest document known to man; it includes many references to flying machines, such as *Trichakra Ratha* (a machine designed to operate in the air) and *Jalayan* (a vehicle designed to operate in air and water).

CONCLUSION:

1. The references and artifacts pertaining to ancient flying machines are too numerous to ignore.

2. Evidence that ancient man flew has been unearthed in more than one country, suggesting that ancient flight was widespread and not limited to one civilization.

Recommended reading

Hatcher Childress, David. *Technology of the Gods: The Incredible Sciences of the Ancients*. Adventures Unlimited Press, 2000.

Hatcher Childress, David and Sanderson, Ivan T. *Vimana Aircraft of Ancient India and Atlantis* (Lost Science Series). Adventures Unlimited Press, 1992.

N O ! When Alexander the Great conquered India, chronicles of him being attacked by "flying fiery shields" referred to the brightly colored shields of his enemy.

Levitation, the art of making oneself float, was supposedly used to fuel ancient flying machines. Even if this phenomenon was possible, it is hardly likely to be able to power an aircraft and carry it for any distance.

The *Veda* documents were compiled around 3500 B.C. and were barely understood at that time. They are complex, subtle, and extremely rich with symbolism.

CONCLUSION:

1. There is no concrete evidence to suggest that ancient man ever took to the air. Archaeologists have found no trace of full-scale flying machines.
2. Man has always dreamed of possessing the power of flight, and ancient writings referring to the subject are full of purely symbolic accounts.

Recommended reading

Anderson Jr., John D. *The Airplane: A History of its Technology*. AIAA, 2002.

Somerville, Barbara A. *The History of the Airplane*. Child's World, 2004.

Wright, Orville. *How We Invented the Airplane: An Illustrated History*. Dover Publications, 1988.

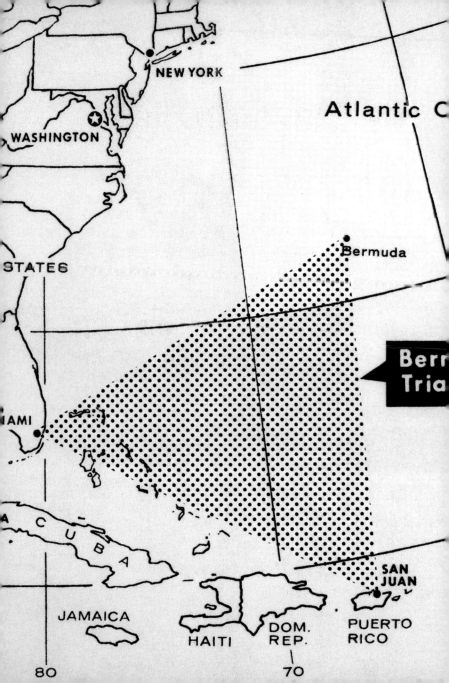

BERMUDA TRIANGLE

The Bermuda Triangle is an imaginary region of the Atlantic Ocean noted for the profusion of bizarre incidents that occur within its boundaries. An unusually high number of ships and aircraft have disappeared within its limits, never to be seen again. The area, sometimes known as the "Devil's Triangle," extends from Bermuda to Miami, then to San Juan, Puerto Rico. Many people believe there is something extraordinary happening within the Triangle, while skeptics are happy to accept scientific explanations.

Are supernatural forces at work within the Bermuda Triangle?

YES! Although the concept of the Bermuda Triangle was brought to wider public attention in 1964 in an article written by Vincent Gaddis for *Argosy* magazine, the mysteries surrounding the Triangle had been spoken of for centuries, beginning with the historical voyage of Christopher Columbus. In his diaries, Columbus recorded erratic compass activity and strange

NO! The U.S. Board of Geographic Names does not recognize the Bermuda Triangle. It is not registered as an official name, there are no files maintained, and there are no official maps available that delineate the boundaries of the Triangle.

Public interest in the Bermuda Triangle was only aroused after Gaddis's article appeared in

YES! lights in the sky when sailing through the Triangle region.

Since the time of Columbus, dozens of ships have disappeared without a trace, and with the increase in sea transportation and the invention of the airplane, reports of disappearances from the air and the sea soared dramatically.

The disappearance of Flight 19 at the end of 1947 is perhaps the best documented of all Bermuda Triangle stories. On the afternoon of December 5 that year, five Avenger torpedo bombers left the Naval air station at Fort Lauderdale, Florida, on a routine practice mission. The weather was seemingly perfect, and the bombers were led by an experienced commander, Lieutenant Charles Taylor. The flight path was over the Triangle region, and only an hour-and-a-half into the flight Lt. Taylor radioed to report that the compasses had gone haywire and that he believed they were somewhere over the Florida Keys. He was advised to take himself and his crew northwards to Miami so that his position could be confirmed. Communications grew increasingly weak and intermittent, and it became obvious that something was desperately wrong. The last transmission from Flight 19 was received at 7:04 P.M.; then it disappeared altogether. Two search planes were dispatched to scour the seas for wreckage; one of these planes never made it back. No sign was ever found of missing Flight 19 and its fourteen crewmembers; the Navy recorded the disaster as having been caused by "reasons unknown."

The Navy's "greatest mystery of the sea" is the USS *Cyclops*, an enormous 522-foot collier that disappeared within the Triangle in 1918, along with 309 crew and passengers. Again, no debris, bodies, or traces of the great ship were ever found.

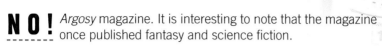

N O ! *Argosy* magazine. It is interesting to note that the magazine once published fantasy and science fiction.

The Bermuda Triangle is one of only two places on Earth where a magnetic compass points to true north, and not to magnetic north. Most modern navigators and sailors know to compensate for this variation; however, Christopher Columbus would have been unaware of this discrepancy, hence his report of erratic compass movements.

The Bermuda Triangle is one of the most heavily traveled regions in the world; it therefore stands to reason that it sustains a higher rate of accidents than areas with less traffic. The exact size of the Bermuda Triangle has never been defined and varies greatly from report to report. Therefore, the number of ships and planes lost in the area can never be truly ascertained. The *Marie Celeste* is often cited as one of the Triangle's mysteries, but it was found abandoned on the other side of the Atlantic between Portugal and the Azores. Many nautical mishaps are attributed to the Triangle when, in fact, they occurred hundreds of miles away.

The disappearance of Flight 19 has a simple and very "unsupernatural" explanation. The pilots, excepting Lieutenant Taylor, were all inexperienced trainees. The weather that day was far from perfect, and the squadron ran into an electrical storm that caused their compasses to malfunction. They ended up miles off course and simply ran out of fuel. The planes weighed in at around six tons each, so when they hit the sea, they sank without a trace.

The disappearance of the USS *Cyclops* has been accredited to sabotage or mutiny at sea. It was well known that the atmosphere on board was unsettled, and crew members had signed a petition of complaint against the eccentric Captain George W. Worley.

YES! Some of the aircraft that disappeared were able to transmit messages shortly before they vanished from the radar. They reported seeing strange objects speeding past or following close behind and often complained of electronic and navigational equipment malfunction.

Many aircraft and ships have gone missing during perfect weather conditions, and no wreckage or debris from them is ever found.

There are plenty of documented eyewitness accounts from survivors of unexplained encounters within the Triangle. Many report having flown or sailed into thick yellow clouds that appeared suddenly from an otherwise clear blue sky. While in the midst of those clouds, cell phones, navigational equipment, and radios have all ceased to work. Compasses spin out of control, and engine RPMs drop off. Many report having to pull away from a strong unseen force.

Deviations in compass readings are caused by magnetic field anomalies, and a high degree of electromagnetic energy is thought to open portals or wormholes into another dimension. Researchers have identified areas of deviation within the Triangle.

There are documented cases of aircraft taking off for short flights with only five hours worth of fuel on board. Mayday signals have been picked up from these planes many hours later and hundreds of miles off course, when they couldn't possibly still be in the air. The aircraft or pilots have never been found, but the incident seems to suggest a time warp within the Triangle. Many survivors have also reported losing or gaining several hours while traveling through the Triangle.

N O ! The Bermuda Triangle area of the Atlantic is notorious for unpredictable weather conditions. Small, violent thunderstorms known as meso-meteorological storms can occur at sea with little warning. They cannot be picked up by satellite and can prove disastrous to ships and boats.

Sudden, violent storms within the area of the Bermuda Triangle often generate severe electrical activity that can knock out communication and navigational equipment. This in turn can cause pilots and mariners to become severely disoriented.

Storms can generate giant waves and produce bolts of lightning or ball-lightning that would look particularly unusual if never witnessed before.

The Gulf Stream itself is incredibly unpredictable and can produce enormous waves in an instant. These waves can engulf a boat and quickly erase any evidence of a disaster.

Another weather phenomenon of the region is the waterspout, which can pull water from the ocean thousands of feet into the air and can be disastrous for pilots and sailors alike.

The ocean floor in the Triangle region is home to some of the deepest marine trenches in the world and is likely to be littered with hundreds of wrecks.

The waters of the Triangle region are infested with sharks and barracuda. Human remains from shipping or aircraft disasters would not survive for long.

YES!

CONCLUSION:

1. There are literally hundreds of aircraft, ships, and boats that have disappeared within the Bermuda Triangle. No trace has ever been found of any of them, and no official explanation for their disappearance has ever been given.

2. Many well-respected and highly qualified pilots, sailors, and navigators have lent the weight of their own experiences within the Triangle to the conclusion that some form of supernatural force is indeed at work.

Recommended reading

Berlitz, Charles. *Bermuda Triangle*. Avon Books, 1984.

Winer, Richard. *The Devil's Triangle*. Bantam Books, 1974.

N O !

CONCLUSION:

1. All loss of ships and aircraft in the Bermuda Triangle region can be ascribed to the area's unique and unpredictable weather patterns combined with a degree of human error.

2. The combination of human unpredictability and the giant forces of nature are more powerful than any "supernatural" force.

Recommended reading

Kusche, Larry. *The Bermuda Triangle Mystery Solved.* Prometheus Books, 1995.

Quasar, Gian. *Into the Bermuda Triangle: Pursuing the Truth Behind the World's Greatest Mystery.* International Marine/Ragged Mountain Press, 2003.

BIGFOOT

Tales of giant man-like apes living in the wilderness of North America have been told for centuries. Stories of the Sasquatch, Abominable Snowman, Yeti, Yowie, or Bigfoot, as it is variously called, also exist in Europe and Asia. The bipedal ape-man has proved famously elusive, and while there have been thousands of individual sightings, concrete evidence of its existence is decidedly scant.

Is there a reclusive ape-man inhabiting the remote areas of our planet?

YES! The cultural history of Native Americans includes stories of wild ape-like humans or "wild men of the woods." The descriptions of the creature are identical to those reported today.

It is arrogant of humans to assume they know of every creature that inhabits this planet. New species of animal are discovered all the time. The okapi was unknown until as late as 1901.

NO! Bigfoot is a cultural phenomenon kept alive by wishful thinking and the passion of fans of the paranormal.

Evidence to support the belief in a huge bipedal ape-like creature is scant, to say the least.

Bigfoot enthusiasts use a wide range of sophisticated technology in a bid to obtain photographic or video evidence of the elusive creature. Their

Y E S ! There is substantial physical evidence to support the claims of Bigfoot believers. Thousands of giant human-like tracks (which do not match those of any known animal) are found on a regular basis. Many of these are photographed, catalogued, and cast in plaster. Hair and large droppings, again from an unknown creature, are regularly collected from areas high in Bigfoot sightings.

Large ground-level nests or sleeping areas have been found in remote areas of forest. Unusual tree damage has been found near areas of Bigfoot sightings. High branches are twisted off, an act that would require two large hands.

A Bigfoot in the wild was captured on film in 1967 by Roger Patterson and Bob Gimlin. Computer enhancement analysis of the Patterson/Gimlin film clearly shows the skin and muscle movements of a living animal. This presence of muscle contraction and the creature's unencumbered gait all point to a living humanoid species outside of our current knowledge.

The estimated stride of the creature caught on the Patterson/Gimlin film was longer than any man could achieve. Compelling reports of Bigfoot sightings continue to flood in and show no signs of diminishing.

There are more than 400 reported sightings of Bigfoot every year. They involve strikingly similar descriptions of huge, hairy, human-like creatures, walking upright and at least seven feet tall. Some witnesses have been close enough to describe a strong, repugnant smell.

Bigfoot is likely to be a surviving relative of the *Gigantopithecus*, a giant cousin of the orangutan, thought to have been extinct.

N O ! efforts to date have been in vain, save for a handful of fuzzy images and highly contested video footage.

Experts remain divided on the authenticity of the famous Patterson/Gimlin video footage showing a Bigfoot in the wild, and in 1995 improved computer enhancements showed what appeared to be some kind of fastener at the creature's waist.

In March 1992, Bob Gimlin himself admitted he may have been fooled by Roger Patterson into becoming the unsuspecting witness to one of the world's most elaborate hoaxes.

In 2004, Greg Long, Bigfoot researcher and author, claimed that a sophisticated gorilla suit had been used in the famous video clip. The wearer was identified as Bob Heironimus.

Hair samples alleged to belong to Bigfoot inevitably turn out to be from bears, elk, or cows.

No bones belonging to any creature resembling a Bigfoot have ever been found.

Nobody has ever managed to capture a Bigfoot, dead or alive.

Many of the plaster casts of Bigfoot tracks vary greatly in size. This suggests many independent hoaxers.

Hoaxer Ray Wallace admitted responsibility for the 1958 footprints that kick-started the whole Bigfoot legend.

The Bigfoot legend has been perpetuated by the vast number of fake sightings, which are due to misidentification of known animals.

YES!

CONCLUSION:

1. Bigfoot sightings extend far back in time and cannot all be dismissed as hoaxes.

2. The majority of witnesses are completely credible and stand to gain nothing from reporting a sighting.

3. The Bigfoot is a rare, elusive animal that inhabits the remotest corners of the world.

4. A rare species will leave behind little in the way of bodily evidence; we are fortunate to have garnered as much information as we have.

Recommended reading

Coleman, Loren. *Bigfoot!: The True Story of Apes in America.* Paraview Pocket Books, 2003.

Green, John. *Encounters with Bigfoot.* Hancock House Publishing, 1994.

Steenburg, Thomas. *In Search of Giants: Bigfoot Sasquatch Encounters.* Hancock House Publishing, 2000.

NO!

CONCLUSION:

1. Evidence for Bigfoot's existence is pithy and consists mainly of reported sightings from Bigfoot enthusiasts.

2. There are no bones, bodies, or clear photographic evidence to support Bigfoot's existence.

3. There are no giant human-like apes living in remote forests, but only in man's overactive imagination.

Recommended reading

Daegling, David J. *Bigfoot Exposed*. AltaMira Press, 2005.

Long, Greg and Korff, Kal K. *The Making of Bigfoot: The Inside Story*. Prometheus Books, 2004.

CATTLE MUTILATION

In the early 1970s, a bizarre phenomenon began to spread across rural America. Cattle were found dead and mysteriously mutilated. Certain parts of the animal, particularly the sexual organs and rectum, had been removed with surgical precision, and the carcasses were drained of blood. Cattle mutilations continue to occur today. Who is responsible—aliens, humans, or animals?

Are aliens mutilating our cattle?

YES! By 1979 over 10,000 cattle had been mutilated.

There are no reports of cattle mutilations prior to 1967.

There are no tire or animal tracks or footprints in the vicinity of the body.

All organ removal and incisions are done with surgical precision (entire jaws have been excised in large, oval excisions, and the bone is exposed and is perfectly clean), and in many cases there is evidence of cauterization.

NO! The scale of the phenomenon is not, in itself, an indicator of supernatural causes, but merely an indication that there is a problem that requires rational explanation.

Every year thousands of cattle die on North American ranges, the victims of diseases, parasites, predators, and accidents.

The phenomenon can be traced to an initial incident that started the mutilation fever, namely the case of a horse in Colorado,

Y E S ! Microscopic analysis of bovine tissue and grass found near the animals sometimes show cellular alterations consistent with exposure to microwave radiation.

The cuts were made rapidly, probably in two minutes or less, because there is no evidence of inflammatory cell destruction that typically begins a few minutes after any trauma to tissue.

Bones were also clearly cut with no bone fragments around the cut.

The carcass is devoid of blood.

Predators avoid the carcass.

Mutilations are often accompanied by sightings of UFOs or unmarked helicopters and occur in UFO/covert military hot-spots such as New Mexico and Area 51.

Some animals have visible clamp marks and multiple bone fractures, suggesting they have been removed (airlifted?) and then dropped from a height. One animal was found in a tree five feet above the ground, and another with its horn embedded in the earth.

Ex-FBI agent Kenneth Rommel is a counter-intelligence specialist who helped to cover up the government's secret activities, so his influential report "Operation Cattle Mutilations," which attributes the mutilations to predators, is not impartial.

The fact that missing organs are related to input, output, and reproduction points to medical experimentation. Pharmaceuticals, such as barbiturates, anti-coagulants, synthetic amphetamines, aluminum-titanium-oxygen-silicon flakes, and antimony, have been found in bovine blood. Pharmaceutical (as opposed to veterinary) concentrations of human drugs are being used on cows. Ears are frequently removed—they, too, are useful indicators of levels of chemicals or toxins stored in the body.

N O ! named Lady, found dead and missing large areas of skin and body parts in September 1967. The owners suggested a UFO connection. Further "mute" reports followed as news spread of this incident.

In May 1979, ex–FBI agent Kenneth Rommel became director of "Operation Animal Mutilation" that pointed out the following:

- The mutilations were the result of predators and/or scavengers. Birds and blowflies leave no tracks.

- Scavengers and predators characteristically attack soft tissues such as tongue, udder, eyes, and anus, rather than attempt to burrow through cowhide.

- On close inspection, "surgically precise" incisions were found to be quite jagged.

- Postmortem expansion of internal gases can literally blow clean holes through soft bovine bellies.

- It is common for the blood of dead animals to settle into the lower part of the corpse. Any blood on the ground is consumed by scavengers.

- The animal allegedly discovered in a tree was, in fact, found at the bottom of the tree.

If aliens were sufficiently advanced to travel millions of miles to our planet, why would they remove organs in ways that seem sophisticated to humans, but would be very crude to advanced life forms?

Decomposition makes accurate measurement of levels of pharmaceuticals inconclusive at best, and impossible at worst.

YES!

CONCLUSION:

1. Whoever is responsible has a huge budget, advanced technology, and great mobility.

2. Aliens are abducting these animals to perform scientific experiments.

Recommended reading

Howo, Linda Moulton. *A Strange Harvest* (documentary) 1989

Howe, Linda Moulton. *Alien Harvest*. Linda Moulton Howe Publishing, 1993.

N O !

CONCLUSION:

1. Most mutilations are the result of predators and scavengers.

2. The public hysteria can be traced to a specific incident that occurred at a time when UFOs were at the forefront of the public imagination.

3. Some mutilations were performed by "copycat" mutilators seeking to add fuel to the myth.

4. If aliens visited earth, they wouldn't use such crude techniques nor even waste their time disemboweling cattle.

Recommended reading

Hitt, Jack. "Operation Moo." *GQ.* February 1997.

Stewart, J. "Cattle Mutilations." *Zetetic* (now *Skeptical Inquirer*). Spring/Summer 1977.

EL CHUPACABRA

The *chupacabra* is an elusive blood-sucking creature that terrorized the Caribbean island of Puerto Rico during the 1990s. It was named *el chupacabra,* or "goatsucker," as its first reported victim was a goat. The creature was sighted throughout the island on many occasions, and its strange appearance prompted mass debate as to its origins. Many believed it was a demonic vampire, while others thought it was merely a new species of animal. The islanders were thrown into a state of panic, and huge numbers of livestock were undoubtedly killed by this unidentified creature.

Is the chupacabra a supernatural vampiric creature?

YES! The livestock attacks began in 1995 when residents of Canovanos, Puerto Rico, discovered their goats, chickens, rabbits, and other household pets had been killed, their necks perforated, and their corpses drained of blood.

Over 2,000 deaths were recorded during the first year of *chupacabra* activity.

NO! Puerto Rican authorities maintain that the killing of livestock was due to attacks from wild dogs or "exotic animals such as panthers," which had been brought to the islands illegally.

Hector Garcia, director of Puerto Rico's Department of Agriculture Veterinary Services Division announced, "There

YES! Every victim displayed the same precisely inflicted puncture wounds which were inconsistent with the bite of any known animal.

The puncture wounds were deep, leading directly to the brain, and were indicative of a premeditated and intelligent attack.

The victims' bodies remained flexible, showing no signs of rigor mortis, and any blood remaining did not clot, but remained free-flowing.

Descriptions of *chupacabras* remained consistent, despite the wide geographical spread of activity.

Chupacabras look like demonic kangaroos. They are three to four feet tall with powerful back legs and reptilian skin. They smell strongly of sulfur and have a particularly unique set of multicolored quills running down the length of their backs.

Blood samples from a wounded *chupacabra* were sent for DNA analysis, and the results revealed that the blood was incompatible with any known species of animal.

Chupacabras have been identified as being anomalous biological entities (ABEs): a species of animal of unknown origin.

Chupacabras captured by government officials from the U.S. federal government and the Puerto Rican government were shipped to the United States for examination. The results were kept secret.

N O ! is nothing unusual or extraordinary about the cases we've observed."

On investigating the deaths of goats and livestock in 1996, police and veterinarians found the injuries to be "classic canine puncture marks."

The widespread panic brought on by *chupacabra* sightings was the result of a social anxiety attack. This is the collective sharing of an emotional experience, and it is a common reaction to rumor.

Some of the livestock attacks may have been made by members of a religious sect.

Humankind's expansion into isolated areas often drives normally reclusive creatures out into the open in search of food. Many new species of animal have come to light in this way.

The creature is a possible hybrid, an amalgamation of several species created by means of genetic engineering.

Russian scientists working within genetic engineering have successfully created new species of genetically manipulated plant and animal organisms.

In August 2000, a *chupacabra* was shot and captured on a ranch in Malpaisillo, Nicaragua. The remains were taken to the medical campus of Universidad Nacional Autónoma de Nicaragua, Leon, where, according to Dr. Pedrarias Davila, biologist and member of the forensic team, "The anatomical detail sheds no anomalous information. We see a complete bone structure, a well formed spinal column resembling that of a canine, and from what we have ascertained it isn't a hematophagous or blood-sucking animal."

YES!

CONCLUSION:

1. A *chupacabra's* method of killing is unlike that of any known creature.

2. The *chupacabra* is an intelligent, vampiric creature whose origins are unknown and whose existence has yet to be publicly acknowledged.

3. Those that have been captured have been closely guarded, which leads to the belief that there is something to hide.

Recommended reading

Coleman, Loren and Clark, Jerome. *Cryptozoology A To Z*. Fireside, 1999.

Corrales, Scott. *Chupacabras: and Other Mysteries*. Greenleaf Publications (TN), 1997.

NO!

CONCLUSION:

1. The *chupacabra* is an uncommon species of dog.

2. The reports of livestock killings were greatly exaggerated due to a form of social hysteria.

3. Farmers, angry at losing stock, hyped up reports to gain media attention.

Recommended reading

Newton, Michael. *Encyclopedia of Cryptozoology: A Global Guide to Hidden Animals and their Pursuers*. McFarland & Company, 2005.

Shuker, Karl P. N. *The Beasts That Hide from Man: Seeking the World's Last Undiscovered Animals*. Paraview Press, 2003.

CROP CIRCLES

Crop circles have been baffling the public and serious researchers alike since they first hit the headlines in the early 1980s. They appear in fields overnight and vary from simplistic circular designs to mathematical formations of astounding complexity. Opinions vary as to whom or what is responsible for their creation.

Are crop circles formed by unknown or alien forces?

YES! Crop circles are not a recent phenomenon and have been appearing in fields as far back as 1678. Farmers have long been seeing circles appear in their fields, but lack of media coverage in the early days prevented the phenomenon from being brought to wide public attention.

Crop circles appear in countries across the world but the majority are found in the south of England, close to sacred sites of prehistoric significance such as Stonehenge.

NO! Many crop circles noted by farmers of the past were simple, irregular circles made by rutting deer. Roe deer run around in wild circles during the mating season.

Over eighty percent of crop circles appear in southern England, near the homes of self-confessed circle-makers. If aliens were attempting to contact us, why not spread the message further afield?

Y E S ! Many witnesses, particularly farmers, report seeing bright balls or shafts of light hovering over fields just prior to the discovery of a crop circle. Many have captured these lights on camera.

Abnormal levels of radiation are found in the center of crop circles. Cameras and electronic equipment malfunction, batteries are drained, and mobile phones cease to work when brought inside them. People experience nausea, dizziness, and feelings of disorientation while standing inside a formation.

By the 1980s, the crop circle phenomenon had exploded, with a rash of fantastical designs appearing all over southern England, attracting worldwide media coverage. In a bid to control public interest, the government manipulated two artists to come forward and claim responsibility for creating the circles. Doug Bower and Dave Chorley from Hampshire, England, claimed they had made all the crop circles using a rope and a plank of wood. Their claims fell apart under close questioning when they could not describe the techniques they used or the location of many of the crop circles.

The biological evidence found in genuine circles cannot be replicated in hoax circles. Plant stems within genuine circles are bent at an angle and not broken or damaged. The plants show evidence of having been subjected to an intense burst of heat, which softens the stems and allows them to bend without any permanent damage.

Crops from within genuine circles have been exposed to some form of microwave heat or high-pressure infra-sound, which boils the water inside the stems, turns it to steam, and forces it to explode from expulsion holes on the plants' nodes. This genuine finding has baffled plant biologists. Many farmers have seen steam rising from freshly formed crop circles.

The plant structure is altered at the microscopic level.

N O ! It is a well-known fact that specks of dust, small insects, or drops of moisture can cause anomalies to appear on photographs when a flash camera is used at night. These anomalies are natural, and not proof of an alien presence.

Many of the physical symptoms experienced while standing in a crop circle can be put down to expectation rather than reality. Human error can be held accountable in many instances of equipment failure. Reports of malfunctioning electronic equipment have, in any case, been wildly exaggerated.

Doug Bower and Dave Chorley were the first "circle-makers" to admit to their art. They inspired many imitators, who have now vastly surpassed them in talent and creativity. Skeptics are loathe to accept that crop circles are manmade and cling to a belief in an "unknown force." They have labeled the circle-makers as hoaxers and refuse to accept that the artists can produce such complex and beautiful works.

Experienced circle-makers know that if a crop is young enough and there is light dew on the ground, then stems will be pliable and will bend without breaking.

Dr. W. C. Levengood, a plant biologist from Michigan, put forward claims that crop stems within a circle formation showed significant and unusual changes. After ten years of study he has now admitted that many of these changes are also found in wind-damaged or "lodged" crops.

Plants inside a flattened crop circle will continue to grow due to the effects of phototropism (a plant's tendency to grow towards sunlight).

Circle-makers are highly accomplished artists, whose many years of experience have enabled them to produce ever more complex formations.

YES! The plants inside a crop circle continue to grow after being flattened and tend to produce a healthier and faster-growing crop.

A genuine circle can be identified by the lack of damage or physical evidence found at the site. There are never any footprints, even when the weather has been wet and the ground is soft.

Human circle-makers have struggled to replicate the complex mathematical designs of some of the crop circles. The geometric calculations have fallen outside human capabilities. Crop circles have, to date, revealed five new mathematical theorems.

CONCLUSION:

1. Although hoaxers have muddied the waters of crop circle research, it is clear that an unknown or alien force is attempting to communicate with us.

2. The anomalies found within crop circles have baffled scientists. There is no earthly explanation.

3. The genuine crop circle exhibits a complexity and accuracy far beyond human capabilities.

Recommended reading

Andrews, Colin and Spignesi, Stephen J. *Crop Circles: Signs of Contact.* New Page Books, 2003.

Leigh, Mike and Thomas, Andy. *Vital Signs: A Complete Guide to the Crop Circle Mystery and Why it is Not a Hoax.* Frog Ltd., 2003.

Silva, Freddy. *Secrets in the Fields: The Science and Mysticism of Crop Circles.* Hampton Roads Publishing Company, 2002.

N O ! In July 2001, John Lundberg, Rod Dickenson, and Will Russell created a huge and complex 240-foot formation in under four hours, in complete darkness, and under the watchful eye of a BBC camera.

CONCLUSION:

1. There is no mystery attached to crop circles. They are the work of highly talented artists who talk openly about their designs and techniques.

2. Farmers charging sightseers to come on their land to view the circles are happy to perpetuate the "alien" rumor in order to attract more paying customers.

3. Why would aliens capable of traveling great distances through space attempt to communicate with us via pretty patterns in cornfields?

Recommended reading

North, Carolyn and Taylor, Busty. *Crop Circles: Hoax or Happening?* Regent Press, 1992.

DEVIL'S HOOFPRINTS

On the morning of February 8, 1855, early risers in a group of small villages in the south of Devon, England, woke to find mysterious hoofprints trailing through the freshly fallen snow. The hoofprints were small, appeared to be cloven, and were found in the most inaccessible of places. They tracked over walls and rooftops, through enclosed gardens and courtyards, as well as across open fields. The villagers were convinced they had been visited by the Devil.

Were the villagers correct? Had a sinister and devilish creature jumped across their rooftops that night?

YES! The mysterious event made national news when *The Times* of London covered the story on February 16, 1855. The report prompted numerous corresponding accounts, one of which told of similar tracks being found every year on a snow-covered hill by the Welsh border.

NO! *The Times* of London was inundated with letters alluding to the "mysterious footprints," and not one suggested they were caused by anything other than badgers, otters, rabbits, or birds.

The extent of the tracks was exaggerated at the time—a common enough result of rumor and speculation.

YES! The hoofprints stretched for over 100 miles, following a zigzag course from the village of Topsham down to Totnes.

The trail of prints was random, wandering in and out of gardens then stopping abruptly at the foot of walls only to reappear on the other side.

At one point the tracks led down to the edge of the River Exe, and continued their meandering on the other side. The creature had seemingly traversed a body of water over two-miles wide.

The hootprints were small, measuring only one-and-a-half to two-and-a-half inches wide. Many of the prints appeared to be cloven, the two parts of the hoof clearly visible.

The prints progressed in a single line, and the distance between them was measured at a regular eight-and-a-half inches. The distribution of the prints suggested a bipedal creature rather than a four-legged beast. However, no known animal leaves behind a single line of footprints, not even man.

The local clergyman, Reverend Musgrove, was sufficiently disturbed to include the incident in his sermon, suggesting that it was indeed the Devil come to Earth.

A mysterious creature known as "Spring-Heeled Jack" was terrorizing the women of London around this time. Its attacks were well documented, as was its ability to spring over high walls and cover long distances with amazing alacrity. Cloven hoofprints were often found left at the scene of his crimes.

Similar hoof-like prints have appeared in other areas of the world; these, too, have defied rational explanation. The Jersey Devil has been leaving its hoofprints and terrorizing the inhabitants of New Jersey for nearly 260 years.

N O ! The tracks were consistent with those of an animal meandering through the snow in search of food.

Details of the prints traversing the River Exe are sketchy, but it is possible that as the weather was so cold, the river was frozen at the time.

Although some of the tracks had a split in the middle suggesting a cloven hoof, the outline of most of the prints was continuous. The odd appearance of some of the prints could be explained by freeze/thaw action or a rare meteorological phenomenon.

The most plausible explanation for the tracks appearing in a single line was given by Geoffrey Household, who discovered that the Devonport Docks had accidentally released an experimental balloon on the night in question—February 9, 1855. The balloon had traveled low over the villages, dangling two shackles from the end of ropes. It was these shackles that left marks in the snow as the balloon bobbed up and down over walls and rooftops. The balloon eventually came down in Honiton, but the incident was kept quiet at the time because a number of windows and greenhouses had been smashed by the shackles.

The local clergyman suggested that the incident was linked to the Devil in a bid to swell his congregation; he also suggested the tracks could have been made by an escaped kangaroo.

Spring-Heeled Jack was a popular myth circulating throughout London at around this time. The "phantom creature" was never caught or identified and was certainly not responsible for the mysterious tracks in Devon. It is now thought that a sexual predator was at large in London, but the stories of his superhuman acrobatic skills were wildly exaggerated due to the influence of the "penny dreadful" books that were popular at the time.

YES!

CONCLUSION:

1. The hoofprints have never been identified as belonging to any known creature.

2. The distance covered by the hoofprints and the variety and complexity of the places they marked all point to the perpetrator being a creature from outside our current range of knowledge.

Recommended reading

Girard, Geoffrey. *Tales of the Jersey Devil*. Middle Atlantic Press, 2004.

Haining, Peter. *The Legend and Bizarre Crimes of Spring Heeled Jack*. Muller, 1997.

Keel, John A. *The Complete Guide to Mysterious Beings*. Tor Books, 2002.

N O ! The Jersey Devil is just another urban myth, and not a shred of evidence has been found to substantiate its existence in the course of 260 years. This myth cannot be connected to the Devonshire hoofprints.

CONCLUSION:

1. When something out of the ordinary occurs, people are apt to latch on to the more unusual aspects and exaggerate them out of proportion.

2. There are myriad rational theories to explain the origins of the tracks, and the laws of probability states that one of them will be correct.

Recommended reading

Lockhart, Gary. *The Weather Companion: An Album of Meteorological History, Science and Folklore*. Wiley, 1988.

Murie, Olaus J. and Peterson, Roger Tory. *A Field Guide to Animal Tracks*. Houghton Mifflin, 1998.

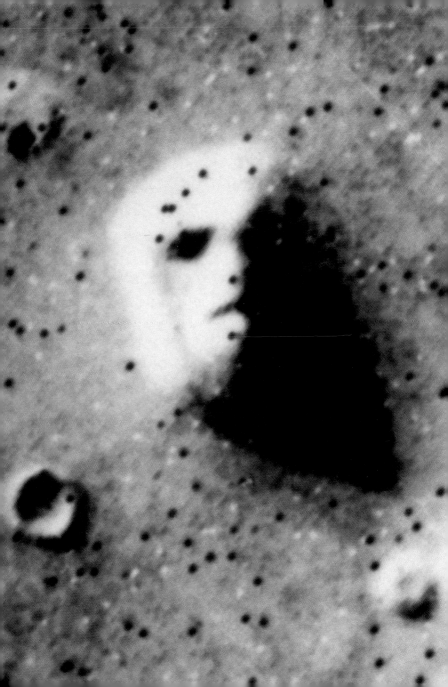

FACE ON MARS

In 1976, the Viking 1 Orbiter photographed an image of a formation of rocks in the Cydonia region of Mars. The photograph, which is catalogued as Plate#035A72, shows what appears to be the outline and features of a humanoid face. The release of the photograph has raised a sensational question as to its origins.

Is the Face on Mars an artificial structure built by intelligent beings?

YES! The well-respected science writer Richard C. Hoagland is a huge advocate of the Face on Mars theory, and stands staunch in his conviction that it is an artificial structure. He boasts an impressive list of achievements within the history of space exploration and has been invited to brief NASA at least four times since 1988 on the results of his ongoing "Cydonia investigation."

The image of the "face" appeared on two separate

NO! Science writer Richard Hoagland's invitations to brief NASA on his Cydonia investigations were not as impressive as they sound. The "talks" were more for entertainment purposes, an employee perk, and not serious examinations of his ideas. His most notable contribution to the history of space exploration was a suggestion to put a message aboard the space probes Pioneer 10 and 11. The messages were intended for alien life-

Y E S ! frames of the Viking 1 scans. Although each image was photographed when the sun was at a different angle, the features and structures of the face remained the same. It was clear the anomaly was not just a play of light and shadow.

The features on the face are bilaterally symmetrical. This type of symmetry is highly unlikely in a natural formation.

The original NASA pictures were enhanced and cleaned up by experts of electrical engineering and digital imaging processing. The refined results were astounding, highlighting previously unseen details such as teeth, irises, and the outline of a headdress.

Digital enhancement also produced three-dimensional views of the "face," which lent further credence to the artificial structure theory.

Additional images on the photographs were even more impressive than the "face." A five-sided pyramid over two miles wide can be seen situated exactly 1/360th of the Martian polar diameter away from the face. It displays pentagonal and hexagonal geometry and has bilateral symmetry.

The remains of structures bearing a striking resemblance to a city complex can be seen lying in a position perpendicular to the pyramid. The arrangement of the "face," the city, and the pyramid form a perfect equilateral triangle.

Similarities between the Cydonia pyramid and the great pyramids of Egypt are astonishing, as are the similarities between the features on the "face" and images of Egyptian sphinxes. If there is a connection, the implications are staggering.

In the spring of 1998 a new orbiter, the Mars Global Surveyor (MGS), was on track to reach Mars to continue mapping the surface, but with much higher-resolution equipment. Only after a public outcry

N O ! forms, should they stumble upon the probes in outer space.

The fact that the outcrop of rocks in the Cydonia area resembles a human face is purely coincidental. The human brain is particularly adept at recognizing patterns and shapes that are familiar. We quite often see facial features in clouds, fires, or in oddly-shaped vegetables.

The face is purported to exhibit bilateral symmetry, which is most often found in artificial structures. However bilateral symmetry also occurs throughout nature; most animals, plants, and insects are bilaterally symmetrical. Natural geological formations can also be bilaterally symmetrical; it is not as common, but it does occur.

The Viking Orbiter photographs had an image resolution of roughly 460 square feet per pixel. Anything smaller would not have registered on the photo, so there can have been no details of irises or teeth on the face.

Once people began to entertain the possibility of there being a face on Mars, they actively looked for other anomalies. When you look for something intensively enough you will invariably find it, even if it doesn't exist in the first place.

An image of an anomalous "pyramid" shows a lumpy shape and nothing that could be described as geometric. When you take into account the image resolution of 460 square feet per pixel, this lack of geometry becomes even more apparent. The same can be said of a mass of rocks reported to be the remains of a city.

Any mention of a pyramid immediately brings Egypt to mind, but as there is no pyramid on Mars, there can be no connection.

NASA scientists were aware that the Cydonia images were simply an amusing coincidence of light and shadow, so when the Mars

YES! did NASA agree to re-photograph the Cydonia area and verify the "face."

NASA must be aware of the significance of their discovery but are refusing to give scientists the opportunity to perform a serious study of the evidence. Subsequent photographs of the Cydonia area are few and have been doctored to disguise the features. We are now only fed what they want us to see.

CONCLUSION:

1. The "Face on Mars" is possibly the most profound discovery in human history and cannot be ignored.

2. The structures on Mars are undoubtedly of artificial origin. Their construction is far too precise and geometrical to be a natural occurrence.

3. It is vital that new manned space explorations further investigate this extraordinary stone face.

Recommended reading

Hancock, Graham. *The Mars Mystery.* Three Rivers Press, 1999.

Hoagland, Richard C. *The Monuments of Mars: A City on the Edge of Forever.* North Atlantic Books; 5th edition, 2001.

McDaniel, Stanley V. *The Case for the Face: Scientists Examine the Evidence for Alien Artifacts on Mars.* Adventures Unlimited Press, 1998.

N O ! Global Surveyor (MGS) began collecting new images of the planet's surface, the Cydonia region was not a priority, as there were other areas that were of more geological interest.

The photographs sent from the MGS in June 2002 had an image resolution at least ten times greater than the Viking photos and categorically showed that the Face on Mars was nothing more than a "normal geologic feature with slopes and ridges carved by eons of wind and downslope motion due to gravity."

As the Face on Mars has been proved to be nothing more than light, shadow, and grainy photographic images, there is no way that NASA would spend millions of dollars on investigations just to prove it all over again.

CONCLUSION:

1. The photographs sent back from the MGS have irrefutably shown that there are no artificial structures on Mars.

2. The MGS continuously sends back images from the surface of Mars, most of which can be accessed via the Internet. There are plenty of astonishing images of craters, volcanoes, sand dunes, and chasms, but none that remotely resemble a face.

Recommended reading

Croswell, Ken. *Magnificent Mars*. Free Press, 2003.

Hanlon, Michael. *The Real Mars*. Carroll & Graf, 2004.

Hartman, William K. *A Traveler's Guide to Mars*. Workman Publishing Company, 2003.

THE GREAT PYRAMID OF GIZA

The Great Pyramid of Giza is the last survivor of the Seven Wonders of the World. It is the most extraordinary sepulcher of all time and has remained the most evocative. The mystery as to how and why it was built has puzzled scientists and Egyptologists for centuries. Conventional theory states that the pyramid was built as a tomb for King Khufu, the second pharaoh of the fourth dynasty. This accepted idea has been called into question, with many now believing there is another, more mystical purpose behind the great structure, and that it may even have been built by a super-intelligent race of beings who were here thousands of years before the Egyptians.

Was the Great Pyramid of Giza built by a highly intelligent culture thousands of years before the Egyptians?

YES! Many archaeologists have suggested that the Great Pyramid of Giza is far older than originally thought and that it was built thousands of years before the birth of Egyptian civilization.

NO! Ancient Egyptians had a history of constructing tombs for their dead pharaoh-kings, whom they believed to be living gods. The earliest bench-shaped tombs were known as *mastebas*, and,

YES! Ancient pyramids around the world also pre-date the Egyptian culture; this would suggest the existence of a supremely advanced civilization capable of spreading its knowledge around the world.

The Great Pyramid of Giza was not built as a tomb. When Abdullah al Mamum tunneled into the interior in A.D. 820, he found the ascending passage had been blocked by huge granite stones, and when he eventually forced his way into the king's chamber, he found only an empty sarcophagus cut so accurately out of stone that it could not be replicated today, even with advanced laser technology.

The three pyramids of Giza are arranged on the ground in an exact replication of the three stars in Orion's belt. This would suggest an advanced scientific knowledge of the cosmos not available to the ancient Egyptians.

N O ! around 2780 B.C., King Djoser's architect, Imhotep, built the first step-pyramid by placing ever-smaller *mastebas* on top of one another.

Archaeological evidence shows that 5,000 years ago, Giza became the royal burial place for Memphis, the pharaoh's capital city.

Khufu's son, Khafre, had his own tomb built at Giza, the second largest pyramid; then his son, Menkaure, built the third and smallest of the pyramids.

Each of the three pyramids has its own mortuary temple, and alongside Khufu and Khafre's pyramids archaeologists have unearthed the remnants of large funerary boats that were meant to assist the pharaohs on their voyage to the afterlife.

Surrounding the three pyramids are cemeteries containing the remains of royal attendants and relatives.

Excavations have revealed the remains of the bakeries that fed the army of workers. The cemetery of the workers has also been excavated, and analysis of the skeletons has revealed that the workers were Egyptians. Many of the skeletons show injuries to hands and legs, which are consistent with building accidents.

Inscriptions found within the tombs reveal that the workers were organized into groups or gangs, each with their own nickname. As each section of the pyramid was completed the workers "autographed" the stone.

The workers were aware of who they were building the pyramid for, as one of the inscriptions reads, "Friends of Khufu."

Many people who question the purpose and origins of the Great Pyramid point to the complexity of its design and build, and wonder how the Egyptians were able to construct such a building. Egyp-

YES! The perimeter of the Great Pyramid divided by two times its height equals the number pi up to the fifteenth digit. Pi was not calculated accurately to the fourth digit until the sixth century A.D. There is no record that the ancient Egyptians had any knowledge of pi.

The base of the Great Pyramid forms an almost perfect square, a feat requiring knowledge of advanced mathematics.

The height of the pyramid is almost exactly one billionth of the distance from the earth to the sun. How would the ancient Egyptians have calculated this so precisely?

One of the most remarkable aspects of the Great Pyramid is its position on the face of the earth. It lies in the exact center of the entire world's landmass, effectively dividing the Earth into equal quarters.

The ancient Egyptians kept detailed records of every aspect of their lives and history. There is no mention of them ever having built the Great Pyramid.

N O ! tologists now agree that the stones used were hauled up gradually sloping ramps with ropes of papyrus twine. The Nile was used to transport building supplies, and during its annual flooding, the waters came conveniently close to the building site.

Tomb paintings show how large blocks of stone were transported over ground on sledges.

The fact that the height of the pyramid is almost exactly one billionth of the distance from the earth to the sun is a coincidence and an example of retrofitting data. Whatever the distance, it is easy to find a corresponding interplanetary measurement which seems significant.

The Great Pyramid lies in the exact center of the entire world's landmass today, but thousands of years ago water levels were significantly different.

The ancient pyramids were obvious targets for grave robbers, and when it became clear that they did not offer adequate protection to the revered kings, the era of pyramid building came to an end. Future kings were buried in hidden tombs buried in rock faces.

YES!

CONCLUSION:

1. Exactly when and how the Great Pyramid of Giza was built has yet to be established. That it was built by a race of highly advanced beings for a purpose beyond our understanding cannot be denied.

2. The builders of the Great Pyramid possessed intelligence far in advance of the ancient Egyptians.

3. The Great Pyramid holds an important message for mankind, which we have yet to decipher.

Recommended reading

Lewis, David H. *Beyond Our Galaxy: Book 1 (An Account of Alien Existence Taken from the Documented Records in the Secret Tombs of the Great Pyramid).* Science Research Pub. House, 1979.

McCarty, Louis P. *Great Pyramid Giza.* Kessinger Publishing, 2003.

Schoch, Robert M., Ph.D. and McNally, Aquinas. *Voyages of the Pyramid Builders: The True Origins of the Pyramids from Lost Egypt to Ancient America.* Jeremy P. Tarcher, 2004.

N O !

CONCLUSION:

1. There is overwhelming archaeological and scientific evidence to support the conclusion that the Great Pyramid was built by ancient Egyptians as a final resting place for their great king Khufu.

2. The Great Pyramid is a monument to the sophisticated technology, tenacity, and beliefs of the ancient Egyptians.

3. The ancient Egyptians were a highly cultured and talented civilization; it is an insult to their memory to suggest that their legacy to mankind was built by a fictional race of super beings.

Recommended reading

David, A. R. *The Pyramid Builders of Ancient Egypt: A Modern Investigation of Pharaoh's Workforce.* Routledge, 1996.

D'Hooghe, Alain and Bruwier, Marie-Celeste. *The Great Pyramids of Giza.* Vilo International, 2001.

Geryl, Patrick. *The Orion Prophecy: Will the World be Destroyed in 2012?* Adventures Unlimited Press, 2002.

Oakes, Lorna. *Pyramids & Tombs of Ancient Egypt.* Southwater, 2004.

KRAKEN

The kraken is a legendary monster of the seas. It has been sighted by mariners on many occasions throughout history, and it is reputed to be large enough to sink a ship. The recent discovery of the giant squid should have laid these legends to rest, but has it?

Is there still an undiscovered monster of the deep?

YES! Sea monsters have been spoken of ever since man first took to the seas; even the Bible mentions "the dragon that is in the sea."

Reported sightings of the kraken were first documented in the 1500s when Catholic scholar Olaus Magnus collected a number of eyewitness accounts from Norwegian mariners.

The accounts were vivid, describing a creature of immense proportions that attacked vessels and rose out of the water "like a pillar."

NO! The sea monsters of ancient times are not mysterious creatures of the deep, but real animals that have been identified by scientists.

The lungfish can grow up to twenty feet long and has a weird mane that grows along its back. Ancient mariners would certainly have been disturbed coming across one of these while at sea.

In 1806, the carcass of a huge unidentified creature was found washed up in St. Augustine, Florida. It weighed over twenty tons with tentacles over a

YES! There is no evidence to suggest that giant squid grow to anywhere near the proportions of the legendary kraken.

The Natural History of Norway, written by the Bishop of Bergen in the 1700s, includes an account of whales vomiting up immense lengths of monstrous tentacles.

Many sailors have witnessed whales battling with huge unidentifiable creatures.

Knut Leem, a missionary and minister in Finnmark, Norway, described the kraken in 1767 as being about 240 feet in length, with black eyes and a head the size of a whale.

French naturalist Pierre Denys de Montfort was ridiculed in the late 1700s for his efforts in bringing to light evidence confirming the existence of krakens. He discovered a church in St. Malo that contained a painting depicting a ship being attacked by a gigantic sea monster. It was an accurate representation painted by sailors expressing their gratitude at having escaped such an attack.

In 1861, the French gunboat *Alecton* was sailing northeast of Tenerife when it was attacked by a huge body of unknown origin. The crew managed to hack off part of the tail, intending to take it to shore for scientific analysis. However, after a few days, the stench proved unbearable, and the tail had to be tossed overboard.

Witnesses of the kraken often kept the experience to themselves, fearing ridicule and scorn. American statesman Daniel Webster came face to face with the kraken off the coast of Massachusetts and begged for silence on the subject, saying, "For if it should be known that I have seen the sea serpent, I would never hear the last of it."

Ancient mariners were more likely to encounter elusive sea monsters, as their voyages took far longer than those of today.

NO! hundred feet long. Tissue samples of the creature were sent to Professor Addison E. Verrill, an authority on cephalopods. He confirmed that the creature was a giant octopus.

During the 1860s, large numbers of monstrous carcasses began to be washed up on the eastern coasts of America and Canada. Some of these had tentacles up to forty-five feet in length. By the 1880s, the existence of the giant squid, or *Architeuthis,* was scientifically accepted.

The giant squid was discovered to be an aggressive creature given to attacking whales. In the 1930s, a Norwegian tanker, *The Brunswick*, was attacked on three occasions by a giant squid. It stalked the ship and then turned suddenly to wrap its tentacles around the hull. It eventually got caught in the ship's propellers and gave up the fight, but the incident was an example of how giant squid can confuse a ship's hull for a whale and lent credence to the tales of ancient mariners.

Early sailing vessels were much smaller than modern-day ships, often measuring less than a hundred feet; a giant squid would have seemed huge in comparison.

No one yet knows how large a giant squid can grow. One report from a British Admiralty trawler during World War II cites spotting a giant squid measuring over 170 feet.

Scientists have recently recognized the Antarctic or colossal squid, which is considered to be even larger than the giant squid.

YES!

CONCLUSION:

1. The ocean is vast, and a large percentage of it remains unexplored. It is deep enough and large enough to hide an army of sea monsters.

2. Many people are quick to dismiss the kraken as being a giant squid, but as an article in the *New York Times*, June 1992, stated, "Scientists concede that other creatures, perhaps even larger and stranger than the monstrous *Architeuthis* (giant squid) may continue to deny discovery in their vast watery refuges."

Recommended reading

Beck, Horace. *Folklore and the Sea* (The American Maritime Library). Wesleyan University Press, 1973.

Peattie, Noel. *Hydra and Kraken, or, the Lore and Lure of Lake-Monsters and Sea-Serpents*. Regent Press, 1996.

Suckling, Nigel and Eggleton, Bob. *The Book of Sea Monsters*. Overlook Press, 1998.

N O !

CONCLUSION:

1. The giant squid is the creature behind the legend of the kraken.

2. The giant squid is a fearsome looking creature, and it would have looked more so to the sailors of old, given their limited knowledge of the natural world and their superstitious natures.

3. An encounter with a giant squid would have led to exaggerated tales brought on by fear and ignorance.

Recommended reading

Bright, Michael. *There Are Giants in the Sea: Monsters and Mysteries of the Depths Explored*. Robson Book Ltd, 1992.

Ellis, Richard. *The Search for the Giant Squid: The Biology and Mythology of the World's Most Elusive Sea Creature*. Penguin, 1999.

LEY LINES

In 1921, a businessman named Alfred Watkins was struck by the apparent alignment of various ancient sites on his local map. He coined the phrase "ley lines," imagining them to be ancient trade route markers. His observation was to spark decades of debate, between a "New Age" theory and a recognized archaeological phenomenon.

Did Watkins rediscover cosmic energy fields once known by ancient man?

YES! Energy fields are detectable at many ancient sites by a variety of methods. Many people experience certain physical sensations triggered by exposure to this energy, such as a tinnitus (ringing in the ears) or a prickling in the fingers or other extremities. Dowsing rods can also detect this energy.

Dowsing has been able to map the course and the width of some of the ley lines that link

NO! The initial suggestion that ley lines were somehow linked to terrestrial energy fields was not a serious academic theory. It was the product of the creative imagination of an occultist and novelist, Dion Fortune, who used the idea in her novel, *The Goat Foot God*, in the 1930s.

Claims that dowsers had detected energy fields were extensively investigated by Paul Devereux in the late 1970s.

YES! these sites. It is estimated that most leys are approximately six paces wide.

The energy fields of ley lines have been shown to fluctuate, the width increasing twofold at dawn and sunset, for example.

Three key ley lines have been tracked, spanning the globe. The E-Line links southern England with ancient sites in New Zealand and Nepal, among others.

Many ancient cultures perceived the Earth to be a living force, with healing capabilities. Tom Graves, in his book *Needles of Stone*, compares prehistoric stone monuments to acupuncture needles that enabled ancient man to harness the healing power of the Earth's energy flow. He claimed to be able to detect ley lines above ground with dowsing rods.

Ley lines have been linked to UFO sightings. In the late 1950s, Aime Michel's book, *Flying Saucers and the Straight Line Mystery*, purported that UFO sightings had occurred at points that could be linked on a map with a straight line. He called these lines "orthotenies." Jimmy Goddard, of the Straight Track Club, wrote in 1964, "Could it be that the intelligences behind the flying saucers build the ley markers for navigational purposes, or perhaps in order to find readily a form of magnetic current that is helpful to them?"

The appearance of historic, rather than prehistoric, points of interest along ley lines are evidence of what believers call "subconscious siting." This is evidence of the central influence ley lines continue to exert on the modern world.

N O ! He used scientific techniques alongside more alternative methods, including dowsers and psychics. His conclusions, published in his book, *Places of Power*, did not substantiate "ley energies."

Modern archaeology has indeed uncovered linear tracks at ancient sites all over the world. The thing that appears to link all these "straight line landscapes" is ancient spirituality. From the Anasazi people of New Mexico to the alignment of the burial barrows and stone monuments of the Britons, a picture has emerged of the central role the straight path had to play in the death rituals of the ancient world. It was widely held that a spirit would be trapped by a winding path or a labyrinth.

Some argue that to assume that ancient civilizations perceived their world as having a subterranean energy grid is to mistakenly interpret the past from a modern technological stance.

Dowsing has never been established as a scientific fact. Indeed, following the publication of *Needles of Stone*, Tom Graves himself refuted the suggestion that he had been able to detect the ley lines through dowsing.

The linear siting of medieval points of interest is not evidence for "subconscious siting" along ley lines. The significance of the straight path in death rituals survived in some parts well into the Middle Ages. In Northern Europe "corpse ways," or "death roads," were allocated routes along which a coffin was allowed to be transported for burial, with strict regulation about their straightness. The linear siting of many churches can also be attributed to the fact that an early edict of the Catholic Church requested that new churches be constructed on top of ancient temples.

YES!

CONCLUSION:

1. The world is underpinned by a detectable cosmic energy network, in the form of ley lines that crisscross the globe.

2. Ancient people understood this energy and were able to tap into its spiritual and healing power by building their religious monuments and temples at key points along a ley line.

3. It is possible that ley lines play a key role in UFO visitations.

Recommended reading

Graves, Tom. *Needles of Stone*. Granada, 1980.

Graves, Tom. *Needles of Stone Revisited*. Gothic Image Publications, 1986.

Michell, John. *The View Over Atlantis*. Sago Press, 1969.

Watkins, Alfred. *The Old Straight Track*. Methuen, 1925.

N O !

CONCLUSION:

1. There are no ley lines. There are no key detectable energy fields at any ancient site, or linking these sites.

2. There is no scientific information to substantiate claims that dowsing can detect energy.

3. The alignment of ancient and medieval sites of importance, as first identified by Watkins, is evidence of ancient and medieval spiritual beliefs and the significance they placed on linear spirit routes or death roads.

Recommended reading

Devereux, Paul. *Fairy Paths and Spirit Roads*. Vega Books, 2003.

Devereux, Paul. *Places of Power: Measuring the Secret Energy of Ancient Sites*. Blandford, 1990.

LOCH NESS MONSTER

The legend of the monstrous beast that lurks in the deep, dark waters of Loch Ness stretches far back in time. The early tribal inhabitants of Scotland, the Picts, left carvings of all the animals in the area on stone monuments around Loch Ness. Among them was a large aquatic creature, with a long "trunk" and flippers. More than 1,500 years later, no firm evidence has settled the issue of what lurks in Loch Ness.

Is there a prehistoric beast in the waters of Loch Ness?

YES! There have been more than 4,000 recorded sightings of a huge unidentifiable creature in Loch Ness, many of which seem to describe features similar to the prehistoric plesiosaur, with its long neck and small head.

Several sightings involved witnesses who saw a huge creature, with an elongated neck, leaving the water or heading back to it from the land. In 1934, a motorcyclist nearly had an accident when he encountered a creature

NO! The plesiosaur was a seawater animal; there is no evidence to suggest it lived in fresh water. Many of the sightings of the alleged long-necked monster are likely to be of a common eel that has been known to grow up to six feet long in freshwater lakes. How much larger could they grow in the huge expanse of water in Loch Ness?

The eel can also account for the land-based sightings, as they can leave the water and move for some distance.

YES! crossing the road with a tiny head and an elongated neck.

Many sightings have been reported by highly reliable witnesses, including a member of the Royal Observer Corps stationed on the loch during World War II. In May 1943, he saw a twenty- or thirty-foot monster, with an elongated neck raised out of the water. An expedition by Oxford and Cambridge Universities in 1960 reported two sightings of a strange creature traveling through the water.

Many reports describe not only the same features, but also the same movements. In most sightings, the creature appears as dark brown or black, and causes a disturbance in the water before lying still at the surface for a period of time. Many reports also describe seeing a one- or two-humped creature moving at high speed through the water.

Several photographs and film footage taken by eyewitnesses at Loch Ness have been subjected to expert examination. Both the Royal Air Force (RAF) Film Unit and NASA have been involved. The RAF concluded that film footage did indeed show a large creature, rather than a boat, moving through the loch.

There have been many scientific studies carried out at the loch. In 1987, Operation Deepscan recorded three sonar readings of a moving object far too large to have been attributable to any creature known to live in the loch. In 1992, Project Urquhart took some peculiar sonar readings. One of the senior engineers on the project said that there was at least one reading that was "far too large to be one of the loch's known fish."

N O ! Reliable witnesses would be equally startled to see some of the other candidates for so-called "Nessie" sightings. European catfish can reach lengths of up to sixteen feet and are usually spotted on still, warm nights, during early morning or late evening. The prehistoric sturgeon is another aquatic creature of immense size that could account for the legend of Loch Ness. The largest specimen caught in the UK measured eleven feet in length.

Much of the most famous photographic evidence was later discovered to have been faked.

In 1985, the *New Scientist* published an article by Robert Craig in which he persuasively argued how pine logs can appear monster-like in deep water. Craig explained that a decaying log that has been at the bottom of a lake for some time builds gases that eventually push the log back up to the surface. The noise of these gases escaping at the surface creates considerable disturbance of the water, in the form of foam and an audible hiss. After a while, the log silently floats back down to the bottom.

Until relatively recently, it was not thought that a seal population would be apparent in the freshwaters of Loch Ness, but every year there are many seals spotted. In the 1960s, the RAF had not entertained the seal as a possible explanation for the "anomaly" they saw on the amateur film footage from Loch Ness.

There is a weighty body of scientific thought that refutes the possibility of a plesiosaur population in the loch. With sightings spanning 1,500 years, it is estimated that a herd of at least ten creatures would be needed at any one time. This raises the serious question about whether Loch Ness has enough fish to sustain a population of ten or more thirty-foot monsters.

YES!

CONCLUSION:

1. A herd of plesiosaurs have been living in the sheltered waters of the loch since prehistoric times.

2. This can be supported by over 4,000 eyewitness reports describing a creature of similar appearance showing a number of similar behaviors.

3. Scientific evidence supports this theory, as sonar images have been recorded in deep waters that are too large to be any identifiable aquatic creature.

Recommended reading

Dinsdale, T. *Loch Ness Monster.* Routledge & Kegan Paul, 1961.

MacKal, R.P. *The Monsters of Loch Ness.* Swallow Press Inc., 1976.

Wiley Jr., John. "Sonar cameras close in on denizen of Loch Ness." *Smithsonian,* June 1976.

N O ! In July 2003, the BBC used satellite navigation technology to sweep every inch of Loch Ness with sonar. Their team reported, "We went from shoreline to shoreline, top to bottom on this one, we have covered everything in this loch and we saw no signs of any large living animal in the loch."

CONCLUSION:

1. There are no plesiosaurs in Loch Ness. They were not freshwater animals, and, in any case, the fish population in the loch is not sufficient to sustain any large aquatic predator.

2. The (genuine) sightings of moving creatures are likely to be seals, large fish, or eels.

3. Pine logs that have been on the bed of deep water for some time account for many sightings of a long, thin, brown/black creature, appearing motionless at the surface before slipping gently back below. Underwater waves caused by seismic activity may also account for many sightings.

4. The most recent scientific studies using sonar equipment have failed to pinpoint any large animal in the loch.

Recommended reading

Binns, R. *The Loch Ness Mystery Solved*. Open Books, 1984.

Burton, M. *The Elusive Monster*. Rupert Hart-Davis, 1961.

Squatriglia, Chuck. "Mystery Unlocked? A Scientist Says He's Solved a Monster Controversy." *San Francisco Chronicle,* June 27, 2001.

MOON LANDING

On July 20, 1969, two American astronauts from the Apollo 11 mission set foot on the moon. They spent twenty-one hours on the lunar surface and collected forty-six pounds of lunar rocks. But some believe that NASA technology in the 1960s wasn't up to the task of a real moon landing and that the entire mission was an elaborate hoax, designed to win the Cold War, that has conned the world for over thirty-five years.

Was the moon landing faked?

YES! NASA faked the moon landings to fulfill John F. Kennedy's challenge to put men on the moon by the end of the 1960s, thus beating the Russians.

NO! If the moon landings were faked, you can be sure the Russians would have been able to tell better than anyone, and they wouldn't have kept it quiet, either.

If Neil Armstrong was the first astronaut to walk on the surface of the moon, who filmed him climbing down the ladder?

Armstrong was the first man on the moon. He was filmed by a video camera attached to the side of the landing module.

There's no gravity on the moon, so why didn't the astronauts just float away?

The gravitational pull of the moon is one-sixth that on Earth, and the astronauts had weighted boots, which explains why they didn't float away.

YES! Why did the astronauts' boots leave footprints in the dry lunar sand?

If there is only one light source, the sun, why do many photos show shadows at different angles? This proves the use of spotlights.

In photos and film footage, the U.S. flag appears to be fluttering as if in the wind. This would be impossible if there is no atmosphere or wind.

The NASA photo-fakers forgot to add in the stars in the lunar photos.

The photographs taken by the astronauts were too good.

The video and television footage were appalling. NASA deliberately made the television pictures poor to disguise their hoax.

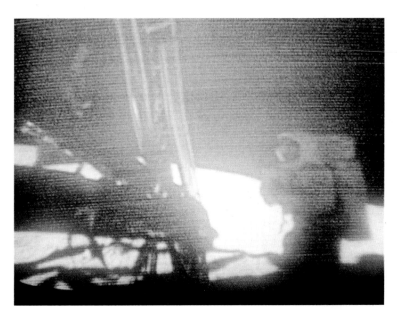

N O ! It is a misconception that lunar sand will leave no trace of footprints because of the absence of water. Lunar sand is nothing like sand on earth, which has rounded particles smoothed by the sea and oxidation. Lunar sand is composed of minute, jagged particles of broken rock from asteroid collisions and will clump together without the presence of water.

The observation that shadows fell at different angles is to be expected. It can be explained by slopes on the landscape and the fact that two-dimensional photographs are a poor substitute for three-dimensional reality.

The fluttering flag was not caused by wind. The astronaut had to twist the flagpole back and forth to imbed it in the tough lunar surface. This caused the flag to flutter. Also, the flagpole was made from aluminum and would have continued to flex and vibrate after he had released it. With less friction to slow it down, it continued to flutter for a long time.

The lack of stars in the footage is not suspicious. The cameras and films the Apollo missions took with them were designed to photograph activities on the moon's surface. Photographing the bright lunar surface requires a fast exposure, too quick to capture the much fainter images of the stars. If the exposure had been long enough to capture the image of the stars, the lunar surface images would be overexposed blobs.

The quality of the photographs taken on the moon is partly the result of the extensive photographic training the astronauts received prior to the mission. The cameras were designed by Hasselblad to be used by astronauts wearing cumbersome space suits. The Apollo astronauts took around 17,000 photographs on the lunar surface. The useless photos just haven't been published. Not surprisingly, NASA published only the best photos.

YES! The crosshairs on some photographs appear to go behind the objects in the photograph.

The Van Allen belt is a band of high-energy particles trapped in the Earth's magnetic field. Radiation from these belts would kill any astronaut passing through them.

CONCLUSION:

1. The moon landings were faked in order to convince the Russians of U.S. technological supremacy. Any NASA whistle-blowers have been eliminated.

2. The hoax is indicated by the numerous errors made in the production of photographic and film footage.

3. The physical evidence of the astronauts' presence at the scene of the hoax, namely the footprints, shadows, and movements of the flag, preclude any genuine moon landing.

Recommended reading

Bennett, Mary D. *Dark Moon: Apollo and the Whistle-Blowers.* Aulis Publishers, 1998.

Kaysing, Bill. *We Never Went to the Moon.* Society of Metaphysicians Ltd., 1999.

Sibrel, Bart W. (director). *A Funny Thing Happened On the Way to the Moon* (documentary), 2001.

N O ! There was no hoax to be disguised by poor camera footage. Video technology was in its infancy in the 1960s, especially when you consider that conventional television cameras were too large and heavy to use in space. It's a miracle NASA achieved any television footage at all under such challenging conditions.

The debate about the crosshairs on the photographs is misleading. The crosshairs are called reseau-lines and were produced by a glass plate within the camera, between the lens and film. They cause a black cross on the film where they block the light from reaching the film directly below them. If, however, you are taking a photograph of a really bright white object, the white, over-exposed part of the film "bleeds" into other parts of the film.

The Apollo astronauts didn't spend enough time in space to be exposed to a lethal dose of radiation from the earth's magnetic field. The Space Shuttle astronauts travel through it with no ill effects.

CONCLUSION:

1. The Apollo 11 moon mission was an extraordinary and genuine achievement.

2. The photographic and film evidence of the landings are genuine and all attempts to discredit them are unfounded.

3. The physical peculiarities of the surface of the moon can easily account for footprints, fluttering flags, and shadows.

Recommended reading

Plait, Philip C. *Bad Astronomy: Misconceptions and Misuses Revealed, from Astrology to the Moon Landing Hoax.* John Wiley & Sons Inc., 2002.

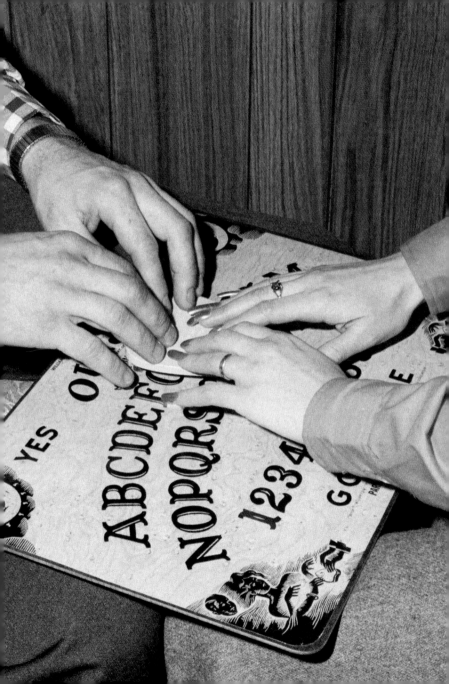

OUIJA BOARD

The Ouija board is covered with the letters of the alphabet and a few simple words, such as "yes," "no," and "goodbye." Many believe the board is a tool through which the spirits of the dead can communicate with the living. Skeptics argue that any such communications are straight from the unconscious minds of those using the board.

Can the Ouija board make contact with the dead?

YES! The Ouija board has been used to make contact with the spirits of the dead for more than two millennia. The origins of the Ouija board date back to ancient times—Pythagoras in Greece in the sixth century B.C. and the Byzantine historian Ammianus Marcellinus in the fourth century. Also, in ancient Chinese civilizations, early variations on the modern Ouija board were described.

There are several cases of highly positive relationships that have been built up between

NO! There is no firm evidence to substantiate the claim that the origins of the modern Ouija board date back to ancient times. Scholars who have written about Pythagoras have not mentioned anything resembling the board. This is a myth originating from a book by Lewis Spence written in 1920, *An Encyclopedia of Occultism*. Spence described a "mystic table" used by Pythagoras but did not specify his sources.

The Ouija method, in fact, originated with two sisters from New York who, in 1848, claimed

YES! a living and a deceased soul via the Ouija. The most intriguing of these are the examples of literary spirits. In 1912, an American woman named Pearl Curran communicated with the spirit of Patience Worth, who said she had been born in Dorset, England, in 1642. Over seven years, Patience dictated five novels and countless poems to Pearl through the board. The *New York Times* described one of her novels as having been "constructed with the precision and accuracy of a master hand." One of her poems won first prize in an all-American poetry competition.

Leading psychics explain that the Ouija has addictive properties for some, especially more weak-minded users. In these cases the user is left vulnerable to repeated contact with what can be malevolent spirits. These spirits are enabled to make contact with the user at any time, with or without the board. The person will be fed ideas in the form of an inner "voice." Paul Beard, president of the College of Psychic Studies in the UK, described this phenomenon in his book, *A Field of Enquiry: The College of Psychic Studies*, warning that overuse of the board risks exposure to "practically continuous evil suggestions."

There are many cases of respectable people using the Ouija board and getting messages through that are full of foul obscenities and violent threats of a kind that no party using the board would ever use. Mediums everywhere have long experience of spirits of the recently dead who are resentful of the living.

The Ouija has often been known to provide insight into the future and is a tool often used as a means of divination. Many skeptics have been convinced in this way. Martin Ebon, in *The Satan Trap*, tells how his skepticism changed to astonishment when a session with the Ouija board made several highly accurate predictions, including warning that New York would flood in 1973.

N O ! they were mediums, posing questions to the dead, who responded with "taps" on the furniture. Three decades later, the Fox sisters admitted their deception: the taps had been the cracking of their toes. The modern séance was born from the deceit, and the Ouija swiftly followed.

Writers and publishers often search for the "unique selling point" that will help promote their book. How better to market books discussing the afterlife, reincarnation, and all things spiritual than to write under the pretext of a genuine "ghost writer"?

The real secret behind the Ouija board lies in its power to tap into the unconscious mind of one or more of the players. Many have tested this theory satisfactorily by carrying out literal "blind trials." Reliably, the board will produce unintelligible gibberish if all participants are blindfolded. A psychological factor known as the "ideomotor effect" explains the imperceptible movements of participants' hands. It is this that will act as a catalyst for anyone with a predisposition to mental illness.

The unconscious mind often harbors the most unpleasant of thoughts, even of the most respectable person. The Ouija provides a "safe" means of venting the most violent and offensive thoughts that lurk in our subconscious.

Cold-reading techniques are widely accepted as a deft method of tricking a subject into believing a person has mystical powers of telepathy or divination. Many professional entertainers rely upon this technique, as it persuades a willing audience that their words have much more significance than they actually do.

YES!

CONCLUSION:

1. The Ouija enables the living to make contact with the spirits of the dead, with or without the intervention of a medium.

2. The Ouija has a long history. If it is not a genuine method of spirit contact, why has it survived so long?

3. The power and danger of the Ouija, if not handled properly, has resulted in many well-documented cases of mental illness.

4. The Ouija provides access to information that no living soul could possess. It has foretold the future, answered questions, and even dictated best-selling works of literature.

Recommended reading

Beard, Paul. *Field of Enquiry: The College of Psychic Studies*. College of Psychic Studies, 1971.

Cace, Hugh Lyn. *Venture Inward: Edgar Cayce's Story and the Mysteries of the Unconscious Mind*. A.R.E. Press, 1996.

Gross, Edmund. *The Ouija Board: A Doorway to the Occult*. P & R Publishing, 1994.

Roberts, Virginia Kent. *My Friend, the Ouija Board*. Brite Lite Books, 2003.

N O !

CONCLUSION:

1. The Ouija cannot establish any contact with the spirits of the dead. Any communication that has not been consciously provided by one of the participants has been unconsciously provided.

2. Cases of mental disorder or spirit possession are the psychological consequences of an already unstable individual meddling with their unconscious mind via the Ouija board.

3. The apparent divination qualities of the board are also a con; cold-reading techniques produce identical results in stage shows the world over.

Recommended reading

Barrieau, Larry. "Ouija in the Classroom." *Skeptical Briefs Newsletter*, September 1997.

Hoffman, Basil. *Cold Reading and How to Be Good at It*. Dramaline Publications, 1999.

Milbourne, Christopher. *ESP, Seers & Psychics*. Thomas Y. Crowell Co., 1970.

THE PHILADELPHIA EXPERIMENT

In 1955, amateur astronomer Morris Jessup received a series of letters from Carlos Allende, who claimed to have witnessed a bizarre U.S. Naval experiment on board a naval destroyer, the USS *Eldridge* in 1943. He claimed that, for four hours, the ship disappeared from the harbor, and reappeared in Norfolk, Virginia. Then, in an instant, it returned to its mooring in Philadelphia. Soon after, the Office of Naval Research (ONR) received a strangely annotated copy of Jessup's book, *The Case for UFOs*, and called Jessup to assist them with it. He instantly recognized the handwriting and subject matter as that of Allende. The debate about what occurred on board the *Eldridge* in the fall of 1943 had begun.

Did the USS Eldridge vanish as a result of U.S. Naval experiments into advanced military camouflage technology?

YES! Allende was on board the merchant ship the SS *Furuseth* in 1943 as it stood closely moored to the USS *Eldridge* in its docks. His claims were that strong electromagnetic force fields were

NO! Why would a top-level military investigation into wartime camouflage technology be carried out in daylight hours in full view of a merchant ship? The researcher Robert A. Georman pointed out that, had

YES! created on board the *Eldridge*, creating audible distur-
bances and a green haze around the ship. As the noise
intensified, the haze disappeared, and the ship with it.

The experiment went further than anyone had expected; not only
had they achieved invisibility, the ship had also been teleported.

When the ship reappeared, Allende claimed to have witnessed ter-
rible side effects the project had had on crewmembers. Sickness
and mental instability were rife. Some had vanished; others were
dead. Five crew members who had been on the deck had become
fused into the floor of the deck or the metal of the ship. Many were
on fire.

Allende claimed that those who survived were subject to spontaneous "vanishing," a phenomenon the crew named "freezing." Some
men vanished for many months, only to reappear totally deranged.
Allende says that, in some instances, these disappearances were
witnessed by members of the public, including a bar brawl that
came to an abrupt end when one of the men fighting suddenly
vanished from sight.

Another bizarre eyewitness story emerged in April 1959. Alfred
Bielek claimed that he was one of the USS *Eldridge's* vanishing
crewmembers and that the effects of the experiment had teleported
him forty years into the future, where the Navy had subjected him to
psychological testing intended to wipe the events from his memory.

Bielek claimed that three key scientists had been involved in the
research for the project: Albert Einstein, Nikola Tesla, and John von
Neumann. The project was prompted by Einstein's work into the
Unified Field Theory, in which he theorized that gravity and magnetism are connected.

NO! this been the case, it would have been an indication that, "Our naval hierarchy [had] abandoned sanity and historical precedent by conducting an experiment of enormous importance in broad daylight using a badly needed destroyer escort vessel."

Georman investigated Allende following his discovery that Allende's family were neighbors and old friends of his parents. Allende's real name was Carl Meredith Allen, and his parents described him as an eccentric and "a leg puller." His complex story about the USS *Eldridge* was a fabrication.

Edward Dudgeon, a U.S. seaman in the 1940s, explains that during the war, merchant vessels sailing around the Atlantic coastline were required to set a course around the sea defenses of mines and nets. The U.S. Navy, however, was able to take a direct route through the Chesapeake-Delaware Canal, enabling them to make the journey from Philadelphia to Norfolk in around six hours. This fact may well have been the origin of that aspect of the legend.

The Office of Naval Records has posted a fact sheet about the Philadelphia Experiment on their website, stating that they have failed to trace any documents suggesting such an experiment took place.

The ONR also points out that throughout the summer and fall of 1943, the USS *Eldridge* was fully occupied in escorting naval convoys, none of which took the ship anywhere near Philadelphia. Though it did escort a convoy into the Naval base in Norfolk on November 2 for twenty-four hours, the SS *Andrew Furuseth* had already left Norfolk en route for Oran on October 25. Their paths never crossed. The *Furuseth* also never entered Philadelphia that fall, as Allende claimed it had.

The ONR is in receipt of a letter from the master of the merchant ship the SS *Andrew Furuseth* in 1943, Lt. Junior Grade William

YES! Einstein's Unified Field Theory indicated that if the link between magnetism and gravity could be identified and harnessed, it would speed up space travel, enabling man to make the journey from Earth to Mars in days rather than years, for example. This would account for the *Eldridge's* rapid appearance in Norfolk.

Bielek was able to give a detailed description of the equipment brought on board the USS *Eldridge* to carry out the Philadelphia Experiment, saying it amounted to several tons in weight.

In support of Bielek's disturbing story, many researchers have highlighted the fact that Einstein had suggested an experiment of this nature on several occasions prior to 1943, and that von Neumann continued research in a similar area after the war, code-named the *Phoenix Project*.

Marshall Barnes proved in 1996 that not only had Einstein completed his theory, but that he could prove that it worked. He reproduced the experiment on a small scale for two separate television shows, both of which inexplicably pulled footage of his experiment and his evidence at the last minute.

Marshall Barnes spoke to a man named Dr. Rinehart (his real name was never made public), who claimed he was part of the research team on the Philadelphia Project. He believed that the original purpose of the experiment was to project ships from aerial bombing raids by creating an electromagnetic "force field," involving a process known as "degaussing." Previously, Tesla, one of the leading scientists on the project, published an article, "A Machine To End War," in which he discussed a means of protecting ships, or larger areas, from an attack from the air.

N O ! S. Dodge, "categorically denying that he or his crew observed any unusual event while in Norfolk."

The many stories about dramatic side effects of the experiment on crewmen are apocryphal. When asked about them later, they feigned ignorance or gave different stories.

Marshall Barnes's input into the two television documentaries about the Philadelphia Experiment was indeed pulled. When questioned about this decision, one of the executive producers explained that a lack of eyewitnesses to the alleged experiment had meant that the show was not viable.

Bielek's accounts have been highly discredited, not least because the detail he was able to recall significantly increased in 1984, following the general release of the movie, *The Philadelphia Experiment*. His apparent technical detail that convinced several researchers could easily have been fabricated by Bielek; he had a Ph.D. in physics.

The ONR emphasizes that "the use of force fields to make a ship and her crew invisible does not conform to known physical laws." Indeed, Einstein's Unified Field Theory was never completed; despite publication in the 1920s, the thesis was later withdrawn because it was not satisfactory.

The ONR explained that degaussing testing was carried out in the 1950s and may indeed be the origin of the legend, but that degaussing cannot create "optical invisibility." It involved attaching a series of electrical cables to the hull of the ship, which negates a ship's magnetism, making it effectively "invisible" to the magnetic mines that were laid during the war.

YES!

CONCLUSION:

1. The USS *Eldridge* was involved with experiments into electromagnetic camouflage technology in the fall of 1943.

2. The science of invisibility, as theorized by Einstein and pursued by Tesla and von Neumann, was sufficiently progressed by World War II so as to make the Philadelphia Experiment viable.

3. The experiments resulted in the disappearance of the destroyer for four hours and had serious consequences on the health and sanity of its crew.

4. During those four hours, the crew was transported to Norfolk, Virginia, and some found themselves teleported forty years into the future.

Recommended reading

Moore, William and Berlitz, Charles. *The Philadelphia Experiment: Project Invisibility*, First Ed. 1979. Fawcett, 1995.

Steiger, Brad. *The Philadelphia Experiment and Other UFO Conspiracies.* Inner Light Global Communications, 1990.

Swartz, Tim and Beckley, Timothy (editor). *The Lost Journals of Nikola Tesla.* Inner Light Publications & Global Communications, 2000.

N O !

CONCLUSION:

1. The USS *Eldridge* was never in Philadelphia harbor in the fall of 1943 and was never the scene for experiments into invisibility.

2. Carl Allen (a.k.a. Allende) fabricated his stories. The SS *Andrew Furuseth* was not in Philadelphia in the fall of 1943 and saw nothing unusual during its period in Norfolk.

3. The "science of invisibility" is based on an incomplete theory of Albert Einstein.

4. There was no Philadelphia Experiment.

Recommended reading

Georman, Robert A. "Alias Carlos Allende: The Mystery Man Behind the Philadelphia Experiment." *Fate*, October 1980.

Vallee, Jacques F. "Anatomy of a Hoax: The Philadelphia Experiment 50 Years Later." *Journal of Scientific Exploration*, Spring 1994.

SPEAKING IN TONGUES

Speaking in tongues is a phenomenon in which an individual begins to talk in a language that is not their own and of which they have no prior knowledge. It is most often, but not always, experienced while in a state of religious ecstasy or deep prayer, and there are two different forms. The first is known as glossolalia, in which the tongue heard bears no correspondence with any human language. The second, xenoglossia, describes speaking in a recognized foreign language unknown to the individual.

Is it possible to spontaneously speak in an unknown tongue?

YES! Speaking in tongues is a divine gift and is regarded as an integral part of the Charismatic and Pentecostal Christian movement. It is the Holy Spirit speaking through the individual directly to God. There are over four million people in the United States alone who are able to speak in tongues.

NO! St. Paul made it clear in Corinthians that the gift of tongues was a temporary one, saying that, at some point, it would no longer be bestowed upon believers. Cases only really began to be reported again after the Charismatic revival in the 1960s and 1970s.

Even within Christian churches there is disagreement about the authenticity of tongues as a

YES! Glossolalia is the language of angels. It is a heavenly tongue that is unintelligible to the average person.

Usually within a congregation, where someone has been granted the gift of tongues, someone else is granted the gift of translation. Most commonly, the translation is not possible to the person talking.

Glossolalia was a common feature of the early church.

Speaking in tongues first appears in the Bible at the Tower of Babel, where people gained the power of speaking in unknown languages, thereby losing the ability to understand each other.

St. Paul is the biblical authority on glossolalia. In his letters to the Corinthians, he refers to the "tongues of angels." He provides the church at Corinth with instruction about the gift of tongues. He recommends that, during a service, the number of people speaking in tongues should be limited to three at most. And unless someone within the congregation has the ability to translate, he suggests everybody else remain silent.

The apostles themselves were the first Christian xenoglossics. At Pentecost they were filled with the Holy Spirit, which appeared in the form of a flame above their heads, and bestowed upon them the gift of tongues. The assembled gathering consisted of people from many countries. Everyone was able to understand the apostles as they spoke.

Glossolalia has been scientifically studied by linguists and social anthropologists. In many cases, the researchers have been impressed, commenting on the devotion of the individuals concerned and the linguistic order evident in the use of vowels and consonants in their speech.

In one study, researchers concluded that there was identifiable evidence of vocabulary within examples of glossolalia. The word

N O ! divine gift. Many acknowledge it as a deeply powerful means of prayer for some individuals, but not as the direct result of prayer. In short, then, they see glossolalia as a method of prayer, not the gift of angelic tongues nor the intervention of the Holy Spirit.

Studies have illustrated the unreliable nature of translations of glossolalia. When several interpreters have responded to the same glossolalia, they have each presented a different translation, though researchers have been impressed by the strength of their individual faith in their "gift."

The early Christian church may merely have been mirroring the practices of the Greeks, when it demonstrated glossolalia during religious devotion. The Oracle at Delphi spoke only in unintelligible babblings that had to be translated by a priest. This continued to be practiced throughout Roman times, and would have been a familiar feature to early Christians.

There is much debate among theologians as to the nature of biblical speaking in tongues. Many argue that the linguistics of the Bible suggest that it was in fact xenoglossia rather than glossolalia that was described at Babel. As with Pentecost, the apostles were able to make themselves understood by people of many languages.

Greek was highly prevalent as a second language throughout the Middle East at the time of the early church. It may be that when St. Peter spoke to the assembled crowd, he did so in Greek, knowing that in that way, he could be widely understood.

St. Paul played down the significance of tongues, and certainly did not seem to be a major supporter. He was sensitive to the skeptical reception glossolalia could receive. In 1 Corinthians 14:20-25, he points out how intimidating a religious community, where many were speaking in tongues, would be.

YES! "shun-da" has been identified in tongue-speakers all across the United States. This may be a small step towards deciphering glossolalia, but it is nevertheless a significant one.

There are occasions when devotions result in xenoglossic tongues. These are, most frequently, rather remote languages, such as Basque or Albanian. This phenomenon occurs outside of the Christian religion too. George Jennings, a social anthropologist, describes Tibetan monks who burst into Shakespearean English at the height of their ritual dances.

N O ! It is true that several researchers comment on the genuine faith of those who speak in tongues, and are at pains to affirm they do not accuse devoted Christians of a hoax. However, a substantial body of work into glossolalia reaches a similar conclusion. As William Samarin, a leading linguist, says, "When the full apparatus of linguistic science comes to bear on glossolalia, this turns out to be only a façade of a language."

The word "shun-da" may have been recorded in the speech of glossolalics across the United States, but at no point has a common translation been attached to the word. An often-repeated sound is not sufficient to constitute meaningful vocabulary.

Samarin also wrote, "It is extremely doubtful that the alleged cases of xenoglossia are real. Anytime one attempts to verify them, he finds that the stories have been greatly distorted or that the 'witness' turns out to be incompetent or unreliable from a linguistic point of view."

Many times the babblings of religious ecstasy will sound convincingly like some ancient or long-forgotten language to the untrained. When studied, the sounds have been easily reproduced in laboratory conditions. In some cases, the pseudo-glossolalia of a control group has convinced Christian devotees that they are listening to miraculous speech. Linguist James R. Jaquith concluded that it often bears a "superficial" comparison with real language, particularly when performed by one who is practiced in tongues.

Jennings also described a drug that is taken by some tribes of North American Indians that has the effect of inducing belief that one is experiencing xenoglossia. The ancient Greek cult of Dionysus also produced unusual vocal effects as part of their ecstatic religious traditions. These, too, could be alcohol- or drug-induced.

YES!

CONCLUSION:

1. Within a religious context, it is possible to spontaneously speak in tongues, whether it is a known language or an angelic one.

2. Charismatic and Pentecostal Christians believe that speaking in tongues is a gift of the Holy Spirit, and that glossolalia is not a human language but an angelic one.

3. The Bible gives evidence of speaking in tongues.

4. Science supports glossolalia.

Recommended reading

Chavda, Mahesh. *The Hidden Power of Speaking in Tongues.* Destiny Image, 2003.

Pizzimenti, David. *Be Filled with the Spirit: Dispelling the Myths and Revealing the Truths of Speaking in Tongues.* Harrison House, 2003.

NO!

CONCLUSION:

1. Glossolalia is not real language; it merely sounds like it is.

2. Scientific studies have found nothing to suggest evidence of real language, angelic or otherwise.

3. There is some debate as to whether glossolalia was ever a divine gift, or whether the speaking in tongues referred to in the Bible was with reference to xenoglossia.

4. There are no scientifically proven examples of xenoglossia.

Recommended reading

Samarin, W. *Tongues of Men and Angels. The Religious Language of Pentecostalism.* Macmillan, 1972.

SPONTANEOUS HUMAN COMBUSTION

Throughout the last three centuries, a particularly gruesome form of death by fire has left a smoldering trail of debate both within the scientific community and in the general population. These deaths have one characteristic in common: the extent of the burning is substantial, leaving only extremities and a large pile of ash behind. Often other flammable items in the room are left undamaged outside of a small radius around the body, creating the appearance that the cause of the fire was from inside the body itself. In the seventeenth century, people believed this was an act of divine intervention. By the time of Charles Dickens (who killed off one of his characters in *Bleak House* this way), it had a name: spontaneous human combustion (SHC).

Is some as-yet-unidentified force within the human body causing death by spontaneous combustion?

YES! Reported cases of SHC in recent times have provided the benefit of detailed forensic examination. Such investigations highlight the extreme destruction of the body: the entire torso,

NO! Forensic examinations have always established the cause of the fire as an external source of ignition. No internal factor is capable of spontaneously combusting; the body is mostly water. Although

YES! including the bones, is reduced to ash and cinder. This is more thorough than some crematoria, which often have to collect fragments of bone to be powdered by hand, as the temperature required to burn bone is often not attained in their furnaces. Such temperatures are very rarely reproduced in domestic settings.

A body doused with gasoline would undoubtedly burn and cause death, but the body remains essentially intact. This is the case with all known types of burning as a result of external ignition. The cases of SHC do not fit this pattern, suggesting an internal cause of ignition is at work.

The bodies have not been affected evenly by the fire. The extremities are often left intact. A fire of such intensity caused by any other factor would damage the whole body.

The fire is always localized; flammable materials in direct contact with the body have burned, but never those surrounding it. An external ignition would have caused the surrounding area to burn along with the body. Therefore, this also suggests an internal ignition.

In 1951, sixty-seven-year-old Mrs. Mary Reeser was found dead in her apartment. The alarm had been raised by her landlady, who discovered the door handle to the apartment was too hot to touch. When the fire services arrived at the scene, there was no fire, although a wall of heat greeted them as they entered the room. They discovered Mrs. Reeser's charred remains sitting in a chair; her torso had been reduced to ash, her skull had been dramatically reduced in size, and one foot, still inside a black satin slipper, remained unharmed. The armchair she had been sitting in was badly burned, as was the area immediately surrounding the chair. The flooring, drapes, and even the wicks from two candles on a

NO! human fat burns at relatively low temperatures, it would need to be ignited externally.

Forensics have established that most victims of so-called SHC were elderly or infirm, overweight, and often alcoholic. In many cases they were smokers. The fires were started by a lit cigarette or another external factor that caused their hair or clothing to alight. The victims were either unconscious, asleep with high blood-alcohol levels, or infirm and unable to move fast enough to extingish themselves.

Forensic science has also categorically disproved internal ignition theories; in cases of severe burning that have been dubbed SHC, the fluid-filled internal organs are, in fact, rarely destroyed. Forensic biologist Dr. Mark Benecke carried out extensive research into so-called SHC cases in Germany in the 1990s. He explained, "In forensic science, there are no known cases in which internal organs of a burned corpse were damaged more severely that the outer parts."

Dr. John de Haan of the California Criminalistic Institute proved on a BBC television program that, where skin comes into contact with burning clothing or other materials in certain conditions, the temperature is sufficient to create molten human fat that soaks the material and thus sustains the fire for a lengthy period of time. In this way a body may smolder for several hours, causing extensive burning of flesh and bone. This was dubbed the wick effect. A coating of a greasy substance over walls and furniture is described at the scene of such burnings; this is the by-product of burned human fat.

The wick effect does not produce a large-scale fire; generally its effects are to build up an intense heat that causes the disintegration of the body but does not alert anyone else to the problem with smoke. The body will burn upward, hence the destruction of the torso in victims sitting down. An extended leg or arm will not burn

YES! dresser nearby had not been burnt, although the room was covered in a greasy substance.

Anthropologist Dr. Wilton Krogman, from the University of Pennsylvania, studied the case and concluded that, in his experience, a temperature of more than 3,000 degrees Fahrenheit is needed in order to bring about such a reduction in a human bone by fire. He went on: "These are very great heats that would sear, char, scorch or otherwise mar or affect anything and everything within a considerable radius."

The FBI concluded that Mrs. Reeser's body had been ignited externally and that her body fat had sustained the fire. Krogman's response was categorical: "I find it hard to believe that a human body, once ignited, will literally consume itself."

In 1996, John E. Heymer theorized that oxygen and hydrogen, present in all cells, may account for internal ignition in SHC cases. Larry Arnold, in his book *Ablaze!*, put forward his thesis that a subatomic particle, which he names the pyroton, can stimulate combustion from within the body.

Cases of SHC are very rare, but some eyewitness accounts do deepen the mystery. Larry Arnold described how, in 1967, the fire service was called to the assistance of a burning abandoned house in Lambeth, London. Passersby had alerted them when they had seen a very bright light in one of the windows. Fire brigade commander John Stacey reported his astonishment when they arrived to find the only fire was a fierce blue flame coming from the torso of a homeless alcoholic named Robert Bailey. Stacey said, "There was a four inch slit in his stomach and the flame was emanating from that . . . like a blow torch." The floor below Bailey was burnt. The investigation that followed found no traceable cause of the fire.

N O ! where it is not in direct contact with an external flammable source to sustain the high temperatures.

In the case of Mrs. Reeser, external factors were identified and the investigating forensic team was ultimately satisfied of the cause of death. She told her son that she was planning on an early night and had therefore taken two sleeping pills; the last person to see her alive was her neighbor, who spoke to her as she sat in her night-gown, smoking a cigarette after having already taken her pills. Falling asleep in her chair with a burning cigarette in her hand would be sufficient to create the wick effect: a small flame, fanned by molten fat, that, over the course of several hours, consumed her entire body. Furthermore, the sight of a spherical ball of ash alongside a few teeth was mistakenly interpreted as a "shrunken skull" by some observers. There was no shrunken skull.

When paranormal investigators, Dr. Joe Nickell and Dr. John Fischer researched the Reeser case in more detail, they discovered that the fire had in fact spread. The fire team had to extinguish a burning ceiling beam, and other furniture had been destroyed by fire.

Heymer's theories were not based in scientific fact. Oxygen and hydrogen do exist in human cells, but not in a gaseous form that could ignite. Arnold's assertion that a subatomic particle named a pyroton can induce spontaneous combustion is a fanciful fabrication.

YES!

CONCLUSION:

1. SHC is caused by the internal ignition of the human body, possibly by chemical reaction or subatomic abnormalities.

2. Bones are only reduced to ash by fiercely high temperatures of the sort crematoria often fail to reach. Such temperatures, ignited externally, would cause significant damage to a large proportion of the surrounding environs. No such damage is evident in cases of SHC.

3. In other cases of death by fire, a badly burned but intact body remains. This is not the case with SHC.

Recommended reading

Arnold, Larry E. *Ablaze!: The Mysterious Fires of Spontaneous Human Combustion.* M. Evans, 1995.

Harrison, Michael. *Fire from Heaven: A Study of Spontaneous Combustion in Human Beings.* Skoob Books Publishing Limited, 1994.

Heymer, John E. *The Entrancing Flame.* Little Brown, 1996.

Randles, Jenny and Hough, Peter. *Spontaneous Human Combustion.* Barnes & Noble, Inc., 1993.

N O !

CONCLUSION:

1. The human body cannot ignite internally.

2. Bodies do not spontaneously combust. These fires have been triggered by an external source, often a dropped cigarette, and take several hours of smoldering body fat to burn the body in a process dubbed the wick effect.

3. Forensic evidence suggests that internal organs are often not burned, but remain intact, as they are filled with fluid and therefore resist the burning. Any internal combustion would automatically require the organs to be burned.

4. Victims usually have reduced mobility that prevents them from extinguishing the flames in time, or impaired mental capacity due to, for example, alcohol or medication. They have often been sleeping when they caught fire.

Recommended reading

Edwards, Frank. *Stranger than Science.* L. Stuart, 1959.

Nickell, Joe and Fischer, John F. *Secrets of the Supernatural: Investigating the World's Occult Mysteries.* Prometheus Books, 1991.

STATUES THAT DRINK MILK

On September 21, 1995, in a suburb of Delhi, India, there was a report that a statue of the Hindu god Ganesh had drunk milk. Within three days news spread around the world, and people were offering spoonfuls of milk to temple statues in Canada, Hong Kong, Indonesia, and England. In India, the whole country came to a standstill as thousands of people flocked to their temple to witness firsthand this "miracle."

Is it truly a miracle and a sign that a great soul has descended?

YES! Thousands of people worldwide witnessed this phenomenon. In some temples hundreds of people lined up, and streams of offerings were made. Some statues were reported to have drunk over five gallons, ruling out the possibility that the statues were merely soaking up the liquid. Some witnesses have even reported hearing slurping noises.

NO! Just because a lot of people witness an event does not mean that their interpretation is correct. When a large audience watches a magician, they know that they are witnessing tricks because the context is secular. However, when unexplained phenomena occur in a religious context, people are quick to reach the conclusion that a miracle has occurred.

YES! The witnesses were not just simple peasants. In Delhi, people from all walks of life and social strata witnessed milk disappearing from their spoon. Also, many Western journalists documented the event. A *Daily Express* reporter, Rebecca May, wrote, "I had a good view from the side and all I can say is that the statue appeared to suck in half a spoonful while it was held level by the worshipper." Even the *Washington Post* did not dismiss it as an illusion.

The phenomenon wasn't restricted to statues. *The Times* journalist Rikee Verma offered milk on a spoon to a photograph of Ganesh and was "astonished to find within seconds that the spoon was half empty."

Suzanne Goldenberg, a Delhi journalist, reported that "although some devotees force-fed the idol enthusiastically, the floor was fairly dry." While it is true that some of the believers allowed the statue to drink some milk and then they finished off the remainder themselves, there is little to suggest that most of the milk ended up on the floor.

Reports came from all over the world. In the Vishwa Temple in Southall, London, 10,000 witnesses over a period of twenty-four hours saw a small statue of *Nandi* (a bull) and *Shash Naag* (a cobra) drinking large quantities of milk.

It wasn't confined to stone statues. Some were made of bronze, silver, and gold. In Hong Kong, according to priests, a small silver statue of Ganesh in a temple in Happy Valley had consumed five gallons of milk. Most of the stone statues were made from polished marble, which is renowned for its waterproof properties (which is why it is used as flooring), not for its ability to absorb liquid.

N O ! Ganesh is an elephant; the milk flowed down his trunk, but this was hard to see because many statues were white, so any white liquid could flow downward without being detected. Sanal Edamaraku, an Indian skeptic, used colored water and was able to show that this was indeed the case.

Many of the statues were made out of clay or plaster—materials that are highly porous. When a small amount of milk comes into contact with it, it is soaked up by "capillary action" in the same way that the end of a piece of blotting paper can appear to "suck up" a sizeable amount of liquid. That is why the phenomenon ceased after a few days, when the materials reached their saturation point and could not absorb any more liquid.

As magician and professional debunker James Randi points out, the word marble "covers many different types of stone, some porous and absorbent, some not." He talks about a film clip in which he viewed "a small white figure, well below eye-level, that was believed to have sipped up the teaspoonful of milk. In all probability it merely was picked up by surface-effect capillary action, and ran down the front of the figure."

The metal statues are most likely purely fraudulent, with temples putting small tubes in them to drain away the excess liquid.

When a "miracle" is occurring, religious authorities close ranks and are usually very protective of the event. In many religions, to doubt a miracle is seen as spiritual weakness and even blasphemy. Consequently, skeptics are rarely given the chance to examine the materials, and in a place of worship, it is practically impossible for a skeptic or scientist to gain adequate access. The focus is more about bearing witness to the miracle and dealing with the large

YES!

CONCLUSION:

1. Thousands of people witnessed the same phenomenon worldwide, including many Western journalists.

2. Some statues drank over five gallons of liquid, which rules out capillary action or spillage.

3. Some of the statues were made of metal, and the phenomenon wasn't restricted to statues.

Recommended reading

Swami Bhaskarananda. *The Essentials of Hinduism: A Comprehensive Overview of the World's Oldest Religion.* Viveka Pr, 2002.

N O ! crowds that gather to see it, rather than allowing disbeliev-
ers to shatter the belief of the faithful. Consequently, the
only "evidence" is from people who have witnessed the event (and
who were themselves already believers).

CONCLUSION:

1. Many of the statues were made of white marble, so milk could be soaked up by surface-effect capillary action and flow down the side of the statue undetected.

2. Many of the statues were made of clay or plaster, which are highly porous.

3. Some of the cases, especially those involving metal statues, are cases of deliberate fraud.

4. Religious authorities close ranks to prevent scientists from gaining adequate access to apparently miraculous events.

Recommended reading

Randi, James. *An Encyclopedia of Claims, Frauds, and Hoaxes of the Occult and Supernatural.* St. Martin's Press, 1997.

STIGMATA

In 1224, St. Francis of Assisi became scarred by the wounds of Christ on the cross during a vision. The skin on his hands and feet had become altered so that the nails from the crucifixion could be clearly seen. In the centuries that followed, more than 300 cases of stigmata emerged, all but a handful from within the Roman Catholic Church. The debate as to whether the stigmata are miraculous or in some way self-induced has raged for centuries.

Are the stigmata miraculous?

YES! The Bible asserts that St. Paul was the first to exhibit the stigmata ("I bear in my body the marks of the Lord Jesus," Galatians 6:17).

The stigmata are not simply visible wounds; they subject the individual to years of suffering the Passion of Christ. In the case of invisible stigmata, the wounds do not appear; the pious individual simply suffers the agonies of Christ's cruci-

NO! The word "stigmata" does indeed appear in Galatians in relation to St. Paul. It is from the Greek meaning "wound, mark, or religious tattooing." Branding was a common practice among the period of the Roman persecution of the early Christians. Theologians suggest that this may be the meaning of the word in this context, or that it may refer to the scars Paul had as a result of being punished for his

YES! fixion privately. Saint Catherine of Siena prayed for her visible stigmata to be removed so that she could suffer the pain humbly in private. Her prayer was granted.

The stigmata are most often accompanied by long ecstatic visions, in some cases lasting hours and dominating the person's life. In many cases the individual would emerge battered and bleeding from these visions. In 1542, Saint Catherine de' Ricci entered into a twenty-four-hour trance-like vision that was to recur every Thursday evening for twelve years, after which the numerous lashes and welts across her body made it clear she had suffered the scourging of Christ's Passion.

Though many have tried, science is not yet able to explain the phenomenon adequately.

The online *Catholic Encyclopedia* stresses three common features in the saints who have had the stigmata. It highlights the fact that the wounds do not heal, even with medical intervention. However long they last, they do not become infected or smell; in some instances they have a pleasant, highly scented odor.

Hypnosis has failed to reproduce compelling evidence that stigmata can be somehow psychologically self-induced by an ecstatic.

In modern cases of stigmata, scientific controls have been rigorous and have asserted that the wounds were not fraudulently self-inflicted. Therese Neumann, a twentieth-century figure, was subjected to extensive observations. Her stigmata were also accompanied by the divine gift of inedia (living without nourishment); she even entered the *Guinness Book of World Records* in 1979 for surviving on a daily communion wafer alone for thirty-five years.

N O ! Christian ministry. Corinthians 11 says of Paul, "And the traces of his sufferings, scourging and stonings, were visible in permanent scars on his body."

The stigmata only emerged as a Roman Catholic phenomenon in the thirteenth century when the modern-day image of the crucifix (rather than the cross) came into common usage. For the first time worshippers saw visual representations of the wounds of the Passion.

Stigmata investigator Joe Nickell observes that there is no fixed pattern to the wounds of the stigmata. They have changed over time as our understanding of the method of crucifixion has changed. When the image of the Turin Shroud became widely seen across the world in the twentieth century, suddenly the stigmata were no longer always in the palm of the hands, but on the wrists, as suggested by the shroud. Surely, miraculous stigmata would mirror exactly the wounds of Christ, rather than appear in a different form in every case.

Convincing stigmata may be difficult to produce fraudulently; convincing invisible stigmata would be far less challenging to simulate.

Many stigmatics exhibit behavior that suggests a degree of mental instability. Eating disorders, self-harming (the wounds and whip-lashes), and withdrawn, delusional episodes (as the ecstatic visions appear to have been) are common features.

Many scientific studies have rejected stigmata cases as hoaxes or fakes. Some conclude that the wounds are self-inflicted either consciously or psychosomatically. A significant feature of the phenomenon is that nobody has ever observed the full process of the wounds developing and fading.

YES! (*The Guinness Book of World Records* is at pains to justify the validity of all its records, explaining that, "records claimed without unremitting medical surveillance are of little value.")

In some cases, the body of the stigmatic has resisted decay following death, as in the case of Saint Catherine of Siena, and samples of blood from the wounds of Passitea Crogi remained in a liquid form.

CONCLUSION:

1. The stigmata have been miraculous in over 300 cases since the thirteenth century.

2. Modern cases are subjected to rigorous scientific testing.

3. Science has yet to offer an adequate explanation of the phenomenon.

Recommended reading

Cruz, Joan. *The Incorruptibles.* Tan Books & Publishers, 1982.

Freze, Mike. *They Bore the Wounds of Christ: The Mystery of the Sacred Stigmata.* Our Sunday Visitor, 1989.

Ponet, Martha. *The Mystery of Stigmata, from Catherine Emmerich to Theresa Neumann.* Burns, Oates & Washbourne, 1934.

N O ! The scientific observations of Therese Neumann were far from supportive. In his findings, Professor Martini made clear that her wounds only bled if she had been alone and that he was uncomfortable about "her frequent manipulations" beneath her blankets.

The stories of "incorruptible" corpses are apocryphal.

CONCLUSION:

1. The stigmata are not miraculous phenomena. They are either deliberately, or psychosomatically, self-induced.

2. Scientific studies have not been able to rule out artificial stigmata in any modern case.

3. In many cases, those who exhibit stigmata and religious ecstasy have under-lying mental illnesses.

Recommended reading

Nickell, Joe. *Looking for a Miracle: Weeping Icons, Relics, Stigmata, Visions & Healing Cures.* Prometheus Books, 1999.

Wilson, Ian. *The Bleeding Mind: An Investigation into the Mysterious Phenomenon of Stigmata.* Weidenfeld and Nicolson, 1988.

VAMPIRES

There is no more terrifying a figure than the vampire, a corpse which leaves its grave during the night in order to feast on the blood of the living and turn them into vampires. Most of us are familiar with ways to kill them and to protect ourselves: driving a stake through the heart, covering ourselves with garlic, carrying the thorns of wild roses, or wearing silver crosses.

But are tales of blood-sucking cadavers more than mere legend? Do vampires really exist?

YES! Since the beginning of civilization there have been stories in every culture of the un-dead drinking blood, vampire-like entities which prey on the living. Indian vampires called *rakshasas* appear in the *Vedas* in 1500 B.C. Malaysian vampires are called *penanggalen*, a bodiless head that feeds on children. The ancient Greeks and Romans believed in *lamia, Strigoi*, or *vrykolakas,* and the Chinese vampire is called *xiang shi*.

NO! The most prominent vampire legends have developed due to a handful of psychopathic serial killers whose bloodthirsty acts have been woven into legend. For example, Count Dracula of Bram Stoker's novel is based on a real fifteenth-century Wallachian ruler named Vlad Basarb. During his reign, he killed thousands of people by impalement, but there are no reports of him drinking blood or rising from the dead. However,

YES! Vampires are depicted in wall paintings discovered in the Indus River Valley. They are over 5,000 years old and show vampire-like gods with prominent fangs. One of them in Nepal shows a figure drinking blood.

The best documented historical case of vampirism occurred in the early eighteenth century. In 1727, a Serbian soldier, Arnold Poale, was stationed in Greece, where he claimed to have been attacked by a vampire. Shortly afterwards he fell from a hay wagon and died. His body was buried in the town cemetery, but one month later villagers reported seeing him walking around.

The villagers remembered Arnold's claim to have been attacked by a vampire, so they exhumed his body. The undecayed body had moved in the grave, and there was fresh blood on its lips. His clothes were covered with blood, and though his fingernails had fallen off, new ones had grown in their place. Despite having been dead for several weeks, when they drove a stake through his heart he screamed and fresh blood flowed from the wound. They burned the body and scattered the ashes. Five years later seventeen villagers fell ill and died. When their bodies were later exhumed under the orders of Charles VI, Emperor of Austria, most of them showed the same signs as Poale's corpse—well-fed and with fresh blood around the lips. All the bodies were decapitated and burned. These cases are described in detail in a document called "Visum et Repertum" ("Seen and Discovered"), a report written in 1732 by the man who oversaw the exhumations, Johannes Fluckinger, the Regimental Field Surgeon to the Emperor.

There have been several sightings of a vampire in Highgate Cemetery in London. The first was in 1967 when two sixteen-year-old girls walked past the North Gate and saw dead bodies coming out of the tombs. One of the girls, Elizabeth Wojdyla, had nightmares after her ordeal and claimed that the creature tried to attack her while

N O ! Bram Stoker's novel and the hundreds of horror films that followed during the twentieth century have firmly implanted the idea of vampires into the public psyche.

It is possible that many cases of vampirism are cases of premature burial. There are many cases of people appearing dead, especially in the case of drownings. During the early twentieth century more than fifty cases of premature burial were reported each year in the United States. The incidence worldwide must have been considerable during earlier centuries.

Another explanation for the prevalence of the vampire myth is porphyria, a collective name for a group of diseases which were first identified in the nineteenth century. Sufferers are unable to produce a substance called heme, which is an important constituent of blood and bone marrow and is vital to the carrying of oxygen. Instead of producing heme, the body creates excessive quantities of an intermediate product, porphyrin. People with cutaneous porphyria develop blisters and their skin swells when exposed to sunlight. The teeth may become reddish-brown in color and the gums recede, giving the incisors a fang-like appearance. Some historians have suggested that porphyria sufferers may have drunk the blood of others in order to relieve their symptoms. It is easy to see how, throughout history, these symptoms could be interpreted by superstitious communities as vampirism.

There is even an intriguing possibility that dying diabetics may have been branded as vampires in times past. A person in an advanced state of ketoacidosis would be light-sensitive and ravenously hungry and thirsty. He or she would have had receding and bleeding gums.

Some historians suggest the Catholic Church declared vampires real in order to increase its power; they argue that it actually encouraged

YES! she slept. She described a creature with animal eyes and sharp teeth. She was examined by the Catholic priest and vampire hunter, Sean Manchester, who discovered two punctures in her neck. His theory that she had been attacked by a vampire was strengthened when garlic and holy water seemed to cure her.

In November 1215, the Catholic Church officially recognized the existence of vampires during the Fourth Lateran Council of Catholic Church Leaders in Rome.

CONCLUSION:

1. Vampires exist and have been featured in most cultures for thousands of years.

2. Their existence has been recognized by the Catholic Church.

3. Documented cases of vampires exist.

Recommended reading

Guiley, Rosemary, E. *The Encyclopedia of Vampires, Werewolves, and Other Monsters*. Checkmark Books, 2005.

Konstantinos. *Vampires: The Occult Truth*. Llewellyn, 1996.

N O ! belief in vampires so that it could hold itself up as the only authority capable of destroying them.

The description of exhumed corpses as vampires has resulted from ignorance about the decomposition process. Corpses develop blistering, and blood-stained fluid escapes from the mouth and nose. Bloating occurs, which may give the appearance of a corpse being "well-fed." This process produces heat, which makes the body warm to touch. Gases build up in the body cavities, so that when a corpse is staked, the gas escapes rapidly and noisily. Also, blood liquefies postmortem in cases of sudden death, so that a staked corpse would bleed.

CONCLUSION:

1. Features of psychopathic behavior have blended with vampire legends to create a confusing blend of fact and fiction.

2. The Catholic Church recognized vampires to increase its power.

3. The decaying process can explain the appearance of exhumed corpses which have been wrongly been described as vampires.

4. Premature burial accounts for many cases.

Recommended reading

Ramsland, Katherine M. *The Science of Vampires*. Berkley Publishing Group, 2002.

Stevenson, Jay. *The Complete Idiot's Guide to Vampires*. Alpha, 2001.

WEREWOLVES

Werewolves are terrifying shape-shifters. When the moon is full they transform from human into beast and go on killing rampages. They possess incredible strength, and legend says they can only be killed with silver bullets, or cured by abstaining from consuming human flesh for nine years.

There are few people in the world who are unfamiliar with werewolves. But do they exist?

YES! Since the beginning of civilization, there have been stories of werewolves in almost every culture. They have been depicted in cave drawings and the first written reference dates back to 2000 B.C. They are especially prevalent in European cultures.

The first account appears in the Bible, in the Book of Daniel. It describes how King Nebuchadnezzar demonstrated werewolf-like behavior for four years.

NO! Herodotus gave no credence to the tale of the Neuri who turned into wolves. It is likely that they were shamans and took drugs to help them to enter a trance-like state.

A recent theory has been used to explain supernatural manifestations such as witch hunts and werewolf sightings. A fungus called ergot (*Claviceps purpurea*) infects a variety of grain under certain weather conditions. The fungus thrives on rye, wheat, and barley during wet

YES! In the fifth century B.C., the Greek historian Herodotus described a race of people called the Neuri who lived in the northeast of Scythia in modern Poland. Once a year, they all turned into wolves.

France seems to have had the highest incidence of werewolves in Europe. Between 1520 and 1630, around 30,000 people were charged with werewolfism. The most notorious case was that of Jean Grenier in 1603. The twelve-year-old shepherd boy was caught eating human flesh, and he claimed that he had eaten many babies and children. He believed that a stranger whom he called "the Lord of the Forest" had turned him into a werewolf by giving him a magic wolf skin and some ointment.

Another notorious French werewolf was Gilles Garnier, a peasant who killed four youngsters in the village of Dole, ate their flesh, and then howled at the moon. More than fifty villagers claimed to have seen him roaming around during his four-month reign of terror. He, too, admitted to being a werewolf.

In February 1992, the Welsh newspaper, *The Western Mail,* reported the reappearance of the "Welsh Werewolf" following the discovery of mutilated livestock and an eyewitness report from a farmer of a huge beast, the size of a bear, in the north of Wales. The Welsh Werewolf had first emerged at the end of the eighteenth century, when a farmer from the area was traumatized following a close encounter with a wolf-like creature that left his snow-covered field bathed in the blood of his flock of sheep. The farmer had watched in horror as the creature tore out the throat of his sheepdog and then turned its attention to the farmer himself. The farmer barricaded himself into his farmhouse, whereupon the werewolf almost succeeded in breaking down the door, before rising on its hind legs to peer at the farmer through the window, with eyes he described as blue and almost human. A local search revealed nothing but tracks.

N O ! growing seasons that follow cold winters. If the baker in a village used infected grain, the whole community would be infected and suffer hallucinations, mass hysteria, and paranoia. The chemist Albert Hofmann, who synthesized LSD in 1938, did so while researching ergot alkaloids. Ergot poisoning accounts for many individuals believing they are werewolves and others claiming to have seen them.

A psychiatric syndrome called clinical lycanthropy accounts for many cases of werewolves. Sufferers believe they are a wolf or some other wild animal. They become violent and aggressive and howl, bark, snarl, and walk around on all fours. The condition has recently been linked to schizophrenia. The person usually adopts the form of the most dangerous indigenous wild animal—the hyena or leopard in Africa, the tiger in India and China, and the wolf or bear in Europe. This accounts for why there is a concentration of wolf-like manifestations of the disorder in Europe.

A disease called hypertrichosis causes hair to grow on nearly all parts of the skin except the palms of the hands and soles of the feet. This is not accompanied by erratic or violent behavior, but a person suffering from this condition in times past would have raised suspicions that they were turning into a wild animal. Other conditions such as adrenal virilism, basophilic adenoma of the pituitary, or Stein-Leventhal syndrome include excessive hair growth among their symptoms.

Throughout history, fighting men have worn the skins of wild animals, such as wolves, to give themselves feelings of power and to scare their enemies. The berserkers of Norse mythology covered themselves in wolf or bear skins, and took drugs to make them fearless in battle. They were ruthless and unstoppable and would have struck terror into anyone who encountered them.

YES! Wisconsin has had a disconcerting history of were-wolf sightings since the 1930s, when Mark Schackelman happened across a huge wolf-like creature near Jefferson on Highway 18, on two consecutive nights. It stood over six feet tall and smelled of "decaying meat." Late one evening in 1964, a creature bearing an uncanny resemblance to Shackleman's beast was seen two miles away, as it ran in front of a car driven by a Dennis Fewless. Then in 1972, an attempted break-in was reported to the Jefferson County police. A woman described her would-be intruder as a strange animal, nearly eight feet in height, that walked on its hind legs. It attacked the horse in the stables at the house, gouging a long, deep cut in tho horse's flesh. Most recently, between 1989 and 1999, a series of sightings were reported around the Bray Road area near Delevan. All reports feature a large, black hairy creature and an aggressive encounter.

CONCLUSION:

1. Werewolves exist and have been featured in most cultures for thousands of years.

2. There are too many reported cases of werewolves for the phenomenon to be explained by myth and legend.

3. Clinical conditions are too rare to account for more than a handful of cases.

Recommended reading

Baring-Gould, Sabine. *The Book of Werewolves*. Merchant Book Company Limited, 1995.

Summers, Montague. *The Werewolf in Lore and Legend*. Dover Publications, 2003.

N O ! There is nothing mysterious about animal attacks on sheep. A large, aggressive dog could easily behave in the manner described in the eighteenth-century encounters in Wales. Many breeds of dog could be compared in size to that of a bear or a wolf, particularly by a native to the UK, where these animals are not found in the wild.

Not a single eyewitness report of the "Wisconsin Werewolf" involved multiple witnesses. Individual accounts, frequently from impressionable teenagers, are not reliable evidence. The reports are either fanciful exaggeration or mere fabrications.

During the Inquisition, the Catholic Church spearheaded werewolf mania in order to maintain secular control, and held itself up as the only true scourge of this particular manifestation of the Devil.

CONCLUSION:

1. Werewolves can be explained by several clinical conditions, diseases, and cases of fungal poisoning, which have caused humans to grow excessive body hair, suffer delusions, and hallucinate. There are no proven cases of humans shape-shifting into wolves.

2. Lycanthropy is most common in Europe, where the wolf is the most feared wild animal.

3. By dressing in animal skins, warriors and criminals have exploited fear of werewolves, a fear that was stirred up by the Catholic Church during the Inquisition.

Recommended reading

Naschy, Paul. *Memoirs of a Wolfman*. Midnight Marquee Press, Inc., 2000.

Steiger, Brad. *The Werewolf Book: The Encyclopedia of Shape-Shifting Beings*. Visible Ink Press, 1999.

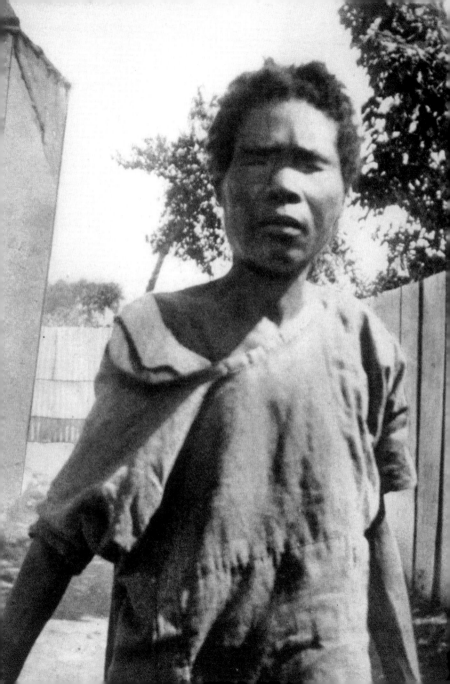

ZOMBIES

In folklore, a zombie is a dead person who has been brought back to life through voodoo. Although it can perform physical functions such as walking and labor, it has no consciousness. Zombies are prominent in the folklore of Haiti.

Do Haitian voodoo practitioners have the power to transform people into zombies? Are zombies real?

YES! In 1962, Clairvius Narcisse was admitted to the Albert Schweitzer Hospital in Deschapelles, Haiti. He was feverish and coughing up blood. Three days later he died. His death was certified by medical staff and he was placed in cold storage for twenty hours before being buried. In 1980, he walked up to his sister, Angelina, claiming to have spent the last eighteen years as a zombie, working on a sugar plantation with other zombies in Northern Haiti. He had a scar on his right cheek that he sustained when a nail was driven into his coffin.

NO! In a review of one of Wade Davis's books, Bob Corbett describes a zombification seminar that he attended in 1989 in Port-au-Prince. He asked the assembled audience whether they had come face to face with a zombie. Everyone said they had, but after further questioning, in common with many urban myths, in every case the person had a relative or friend who had seen a zombie, but none of them had seen one firsthand. As Corbett points out, "Critics argue that Davis grossly exaggerated what he had found in the powder and that he had

YES! He remembered his own funeral, and said that he had only been able to escape when his master died. Several other zombies were found wandering aimlessly in Northern Haiti around the same time.

A Haitian voodoo sorcerer is called a *bokor*. These practitioners of black magic have intimate knowledge of substances which can be used to alter the minds of people. They use a poisonous powder (*coupe poudre*) in order to alter the consciousness of their victims.

In 1985, Wade Davis, a Canadian ethnobotanist from Harvard University, visited Haiti in order to isolate the chemicals which are responsible for turning a person into a zombie. He wrote about his findings in *The Serpent and the Rainbow* and *Passage of Darkness: The Ethnobiology of the Haitian Zombie*. He acquired five samples of the zombie powder and, after isolating the deadly ingredients, he concluded that zombies do indeed exist. According to him the active ingredient in *coupe poudre* is tetradoxin that is found in the puffer fish. The chemical is hundreds of times more deadly that cyanide. Davis argues that while a tiny quantity is sufficient to kill, an even smaller dose would send a person into a death-like state, inducing total body paralysis, although the brain would still be alert. The victim would be pronounced dead and be buried.

Davis has isolated other ingredients in *coupe poudre*. The plants *Datura metel* and *Datura stramonium*, known as "zombie cucumber," and a stinging plant called *Mucuna pruriens*, cause hallucinations and amnesia. According to Davis, the effects of the drugs wear off within twelve hours, after which time the victim is exhumed and fed another cocktail of mind-altering hallucinogens, including atropine and scopolamine.

However, Davis points out that the drugs alone are not sufficient to bend the victim to the will of the *bokor*. He argues that the cultural

N O ! exaggerated, if not lied, about the chemically active properties of the powders he brought back."

Zombies are individuals with psychiatric disorders and brain damage. This theory was put forward by medical anthropologist Roland Littlewood at University College London and Dr. Chavannes Douyon of the Polyclinique Medica in Port-au-Prince, Haiti. They conducted research on three people whose families and neighbors claimed they were zombies. In all three cases they were able to give medical explanations.

The first "zombie" was diagnosed with catatonic schizophrenia. As the name suggests, this severe psychiatric condition rendered the sufferer mute and inert. The second "zombie" was an epileptic with severe brain damage, and the third, who had been missing for thirteen years, was severely learning-disabled, which they attributed to fetal-alcohol syndrome. Far from being a brain-dead zombie, she "asked questions spontaneously, giggled frequently, and laughed inappropriately."

YES! belief of Haiti is such that every person is socially conditioned to believe in and accept zombification as a reality. Whereas a Westerner undergoing such treatment would undoubtedly be traumatized and disoriented, the belief system of Haitian victims would cause them to respond to the process in a culturally appropriate way. In other words, they would become zombies and bend themselves to the will of their masters because they believe in and are psychologically susceptible to the process.

Zombification is used by the secret Bizango societies, which control Haitian life, as a way of maintaining order. Davis interviewed Clairvius Narcisse who believed that he had been punished for stealing land from his brother. Zombification is therefore the ultimate sanction, the equivalent of capital punishment in other cultures.

CONCLUSION:

1. Victims are given powerful drugs that slow the metabolism to simulate death. They are then exhumed and become slaves.

2. Cultural conditioning is a vital ingredient in turning a person into a zombie.

3. Zombification is the ultimate sanction exacted by Haitian secret societies to punish severe wrongdoing.

Recommended reading

Davis, Wade. *The Serpent and the Rainbow*. Simon & Schuster, 1985.

Davis, Wade. *Passage of Darkness: The Ethnobiology of the Haitian Zombie*. University of North Carolina Press, 1988.

Hurston, Zora Neale. *Tell My Horse*. HarperCollins, 1990.

N O ! Furthermore, DNA fingerprinting showed that two of the "zombies" weren't even related to those who had claimed them, showing that bereaved and grieving families had convinced themselves that these total strangers were their long-lost relatives.

They concluded "mistaken identification of a wandering, mentally ill stranger by bereaved relatives is the most likely explanation" for zombies and that "the ready local recognition of [zombies] . . . and their generally considerate treatment might be seen as an institutionalized restitution of the destitute mentally ill."

CONCLUSION:

1. "Zombies" are confused and disoriented people who are suffering from mental disorders.

2. Many returned relatives are simple cases of mistaken identity.

3. Wade Davis exaggerated his findings.

Recommended reading

Brooks, Max. *The Zombie Survival Guide: Complete Protection from the Living Dead.* Three Rivers Press, 2003.

Littlewood, R. and Douyon, C. "Clinical Finding in Three Cases of Zombification," *The Lancet*, 350:1094-96, 1997.

AFTERWORD

The worst that anyone can do when confronted with uncertainty is to close their mind. Now that you have read this book, you may appreciate better that there are many ways of responding to things we don't understand.

All the great scientific leaps of faith were made by people who dared to believe something different from those around them. They flew in the face of all the "evidence" that was available in their time to present radical alternatives—today, many of us take for granted that the earth is round and travels around the sun and that human beings evolved from apes, while heavier-than-air machines routinely crisscross the skies above us.

However, it is just as true today as it has always been that those who open their hearts and minds can see the magic that still surrounds them; those who investigate whatever arouses their curiosity live lives full of consequence.

PHOTO CREDITS